Editor
Erica N. Russikoff, M.A.

Editor in Chief
Karen J. Goldfluss, M.S. Ed.

Creative Director
Sarah M. Fournier

Cover Artist
Barb Lorseyedi

Illustrator
Clint McKnight

Art Coordinator
Renée Mc Elwee

Imaging
Craig Gunnell

Publisher
Mary D. Smith, M.S. Ed.

TCR 3895

Nonfiction & PAIRED TEXTS

NONFICTION FICTION

- Contains fiction and nonfiction passages on a variety of topics
- Includes critical-thinking questions to improve comprehension
- Extends the reading by using interactive writing activities
- Correlated to the Common Core State Standards

Teacher Created Resources

Author
Susan Mackey Collins, M. Ed.

CORRELATED TO **COMMON CORE** STANDARDS

For correlations to the Common Core State Standards, see pages 143–144. Correlations can also be found at *http://www.teachercreated.com/standards.*

Teacher Created Resources
12621 Western Avenue
Garden Grove, CA 92841
www.teachercreated.com
ISBN: 978-1-4206-3895-0
©2015 Teacher Created Resources
Reprinted, 2016
Made in U.S.A.

Teacher Created Resources

Table of Contents

Table of Contents *(cont.)*

Introduction

Making connections is an important part of everyday life. People strive daily to make connections with other people, events, and experiences. Making connections plays an important role in nearly everything one does. It is not surprising then that this skill must also be used in developing great readers.

Connections are vital in developing fluency in reading and in understanding a variety of texts. *Nonfiction & Fiction Paired Texts* helps emergent readers learn to make connections with both fiction and nonfiction texts. The activities in this book also help fluent readers to enhance and increase their already developing reading skills. *Nonfiction & Fiction Paired Texts* is the perfect reading tool for all levels of readers.

The high-interest texts in *Nonfiction & Fiction Paired Texts* contain both fiction and nonfiction passages. The units are written in pairs that share a common idea or theme. The first passage in each unit is fiction. A nonfiction text follows each fiction story. Subjects in each unit are varied, providing a multitude of topics to engage the various interests of the readers. Topics are also age-appropriate and will appeal to children in the corresponding grade level. While reading the texts, students are encouraged to look for specific meanings and to make logical inferences from what is read.

Each unit in *Nonfiction & Fiction Paired Texts* has five pages. The texts in each set are followed by two assessment pages that contain multiple-choice questions and short-answer writing activities. These pages are designed to meet the rigor demanded by the Common Core State Standards. Each assessment leads students to look for and generally cite textual evidence when answering questions. A third page in the assessment section of each unit includes longer writing activities. The writing activities for each unit are tied to higher-order thinking and questioning skills. The writing ideas are designed to help assess a student's ability to respond to a written prompt while incorporating the skills of excellent writing.

Nonfiction & Fiction Paired Texts was written to help students gain important reading skills and practice responding to questions based on the Common Core State Standards. The different units provide practice with a multitude of standards and skills, including but not limited to the following:

- making and understanding connections between content-rich reading materials

- building reading-comprehension skills

- analyzing, comparing, and contrasting fiction and nonfiction texts

- sequencing and summarizing

- experience with text-based, multiple-choice questions

- practice with short-answer responses

- practice in developing written responses to various prompts

- understanding the genres of fiction and nonfiction texts

- quoting from texts to complete assessments

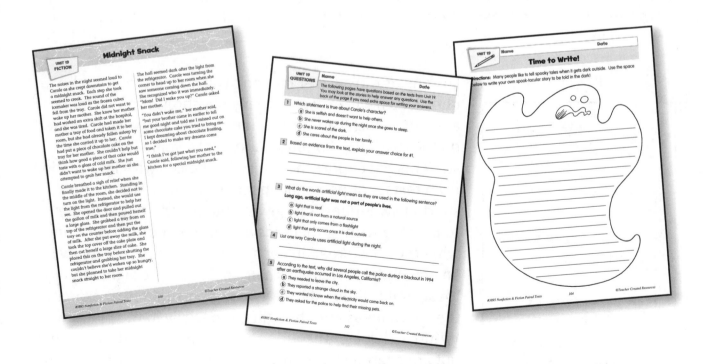

How to Use This Book

Nonfiction & Fiction Paired Texts is divided into twenty-six units. Each unit has five pages. The first two pages are texts that share a common topic or theme. Each unit contains both a fiction and nonfiction selection, as well as three assessment pages.

The book is designed so that each unit can be used separately. The activities can be completed in order, starting with the first unit and working through unit twenty-six, or they can be completed in random order. Anyone using the book may want to look for common themes or ideas that correspond with other units being taught in other subject areas. The units in this book can be used to help teach across the curriculum and to easily tie in reading and writing skills to other areas of study.

Provided with each set of fiction and nonfiction stories are three pages of assessment activities. Two of the three pages are multiple-choice and short-answer questions, which rely heavily on text-based answers. The last page in each unit is a writing page. The teacher may choose to use all three pages after completion of the connected texts, or he or she may choose to only use specific pages for assessment. Pages can be done during regular academic hours or be sent home for extra practice. Students may work on assignments alone or work with partners or in small groups.

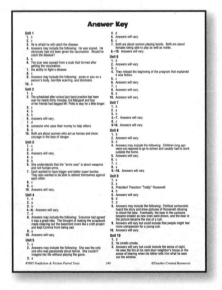

Looking at the answer key, one will notice that not all questions have answers. Many questions require short answers, which can vary, as long as the answers are based on the text. The Common Core State Standards require students to support their answer choices with information from texts, not personal opinions. Completion of the short-answer questions gives students the opportunity to practice writing their answers using information from what they have read in each unit. Of course, creativity is an equally important learning tool and is not ignored in these units. Students are given opportunities to express their own ideas and thoughts, especially in the Time to Write! activities. The writing activities are tied to the texts but are geared to give students the chance to practice the skills needed to be successful writers.

In grading the short-answer questions, teachers must verify that the answers are included in the text. Assessing the responses in the Time to Write! section is up to the teacher's discretion. Each teacher knows the abilities of the individual students in his or her class. Answers provided at one point in the year may be considered satisfactory; however, as the year progresses, the teacher's expectations of the student's writing skills will have greatly increased. A student would eventually be expected to provide better-developed responses and written work with fewer mistakes. A good idea is to keep a folder with samples of the student's work from different times during the academic year. Teachers, parents, and students can easily see progress made with the skills necessary for good writing by comparing samples from earlier in the year to the student's present writing samples.

The units in *Nonfiction & Fiction Paired Texts* can also be used to help students understand the basic principles of text. One way to do this is to teach students to use a specific reading method. Students can use the UNC method (see pages 8–9) to help gain a better understanding of how text is presented on the page and to develop and refine skills for reading for detail. After the UNC method is mastered, students will learn to automatically employ these skills in their everyday reading without having to be coached to complete the process. The skills of good reading will become automatic.

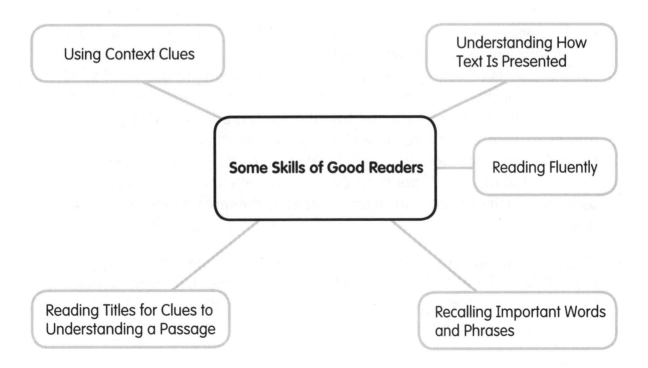

Using Context Clues

Understanding How Text Is Presented

Some Skills of Good Readers

Reading Fluently

Reading Titles for Clues to Understanding a Passage

Recalling Important Words and Phrases

Understanding and Using the UNC Method

U <u>Underline</u> and read all titles.

N Place <u>numbers</u> by all the paragraphs.

C Put <u>circles</u> around or highlight all important words and phrases in the text.

When students are presented with a text, they can use the UNC method to help break down the material. Students immediately underline and read all titles. To better manage the material, students next add a number beside each paragraph. This helps teachers as they go over questions. They can easily ask the students to look at a specific paragraph to point out information that helped to answer a particular question. Using this method, teachers may also discover there are students who have simply not learned how to tell where a paragraph begins or ends. This explains why many times when a teacher asks a student to read a specific paragraph, he or she cannot. The student may honestly be unsure of where to start!

The final step in the UNC method is to circle or highlight important words or phrases in the text. By completing this step, students are required to read for detail. At first, the teacher may find that many students will want to highlight entire paragraphs. Teachers will want to use a sample unit to guide students through the third step. Teachers can make copies of a unit already highlighted to help show students how to complete the third step. Teachers can work through a unit together with the students, or they may even want to use a document camera so the students can easily see the process as they work on a unit together in class. Students will soon discover that there are important details and context clues that can be used to help understand which information is the most important in any given text.

Students need to have confidence in their abilities to succeed at any given task. This is where the UNC method is a bonus in any classroom. When using this method, students can be successful in reading any text and answering the questions that follow.

The UNC method is especially helpful in aiding students to carefully read new or unfamiliar texts. Highlighters are helpful when working with printed texts but are not necessary. (For example, students can use different highlighter colors to complete each step.) Students who consistently use this method will eventually no longer need to physically highlight or circle the text as the necessary skills to great reading become an automatic response with any text. Students who consistently practice the UNC method make mental maps of what they have read and often no longer need to look back at the text when answering the questions! The UNC method allows students who are kinesthetic learners to have a physical activity that can take place during a reading activity. Visual learners are greatly aided by this method, as well. Students are encouraged by their positive progress and look forward to the challenge of reading a new text.

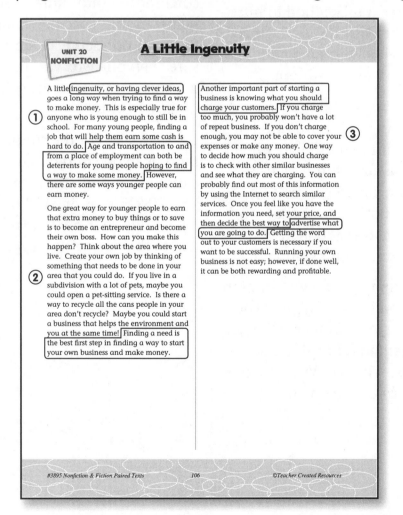

"Why do you have that round scar on your arm?" Devon's mother was wearing a sleeveless shirt. He could see a scar on her arm. The shape was circular, but it was not a perfect circle. He had noticed several other people had almost the exact same mark, including his grandparents.

His mother's eyes glanced down to her own arm before answering him. "I forgot I even have that scar," she told Devon. "It happened so long ago."

"Did it hurt?" Devon asked. It was quite a large scar. Devon thought anything that left a mark the size of a nickel had to hurt quite a bit. He rubbed his arm and winced a little just thinking about what could have caused the mark to appear on so many people's arms.

"The scar doesn't hurt at all now, and I only remember it hurting a little bit when I got it," his mother assured him. "This scar is actually a blessing, if you can believe that." Devon could not imagine that, and he told her so. His mother laughed at his worried expression and then explained.

"This scar on my arm is from a vaccination I was given when I was a young girl. The immunization kept me and others who got the vaccine from getting a horrible disease known as smallpox. The scar was caused from a scab that formed after getting the vaccination.

Before people were immunized, everyone feared catching the disease. With smallpox, a person's body would be covered with horrible sores or pox. If a person survived the disease, he or she would usually be horribly scarred from the sickness or even left blind."

Devon had never even heard of smallpox. He was scared. He obviously had not been given the vaccination. Would he catch the disease? Before he could ask, his mother continued, "Smallpox is no longer something you have to worry about catching. A man named Edward Jenner helped find a vaccine. Efforts were made to stop a pandemic of smallpox by making sure everyone was vaccinated. Now you are safe because others cannot spread the disease to you."

Devon looked at the small scar on his mother's knee and asked what vaccine caused that one. His mom laughed and said, "Now that one did hurt, but it was from falling off my bike and not from a trip to the doctor's office."

Throughout history, humans have been plagued by infectious diseases. When a large population is affected by a disease, people often refer to this problem as an epidemic. If a disease spreads even further, it may be called a pandemic.

Today, many people enjoy going to zombie movies and watching an imaginary virus spread all over the world, causing people to turn into zombies. However, real pandemics are not something that is entertaining. People suffer and die from the spread of uncontrollable diseases. Scientists work to find vaccines or cures to help stop the spread of dangerous bacteria and viruses in the world.

A plague known as the Black Death is an example of a pandemic that occurred during the Middle Ages. This plague was caused by rats and fleas carrying disease and spreading the infection to humans. The Black Death was actually an outbreak of the bubonic plague, and millions of people died as a result.

Smallpox is another deadly disease that killed many people. When Europeans first came to the New World, they brought the smallpox virus with them. The natives who lived in the Americas had no immunity or ability to naturally fight this terrible disease. Millions of Native Americans died as a result of this deadly virus. This disease has stopped due to a vaccine that was created to cease the spread of the virus.

The World Health Organization works diligently to control disease and stop it from spreading. The Centers for Disease Control and Prevention is an organization in the United States that works at a national level to help keep everyone safe from harm. Individuals can do their part to stop the spread of disease by being aware of safety measures each person can take to help stay healthy. People can help stop the spread of germs by doing simple things, such as thoroughly washing their hands and keeping their homes and workplaces as clean as possible. Everyone dreams of a world where all diseases could be declared something that only happened in the past.

UNIT 1 QUESTIONS

Name   **Date**

The following pages have questions based on the texts from Unit 1. You may look at the stories to help answer any questions. Use the back of the page if you need extra space for writing your answers.

1 What does Devon's mother mean when she says, "This scar is actually a blessing"?

  (a) She wanted the same scar her parents had.

  (b) The scar was from a vaccine.

  (c) She does not remember getting the scar.

  (d) She has one on each arm.

2 What do the two texts have in common?

  (a) Both are about the Black Death.

  (b) Both are about the hazards of riding a bicycle.

  (c) Both are about vaccines and diseases.

  (d) Both are about the Centers for Disease Control and Prevention.

3 Explain why Devon is worried when he realizes he does not have a scar on his arm.

_____

_____

_____

4 Write the sentence(s) from the text that helped you to answer #3.

_____

_____

_____

_____

5 What is important about Edward Jenner?

  (a) He helped create a vaccine for smallpox.

  (b) He helped create a cure for the Black Death.

  (c) He helped organize the World Health Organization.

  (d) He is a movie director for a well-known zombie series.

6 Use information from the texts to explain why the smallpox vaccine left a scar on the arm of anyone who received the vaccination.

_____

_____

_____

7 What does the word _immunity_ mean as it is used in paragraph 4 of the text "Deadly Diseases"?

_____

_____

_____

8 What does Devon learn about the scar on his mother's knee?

ⓐ It was caused from a vaccination.

ⓑ She did not remember how she received the scar.

ⓒ The scar was from a bicycle accident.

ⓓ He has an identical scar on his knee.

9 Using information from the texts, list two things that might happen to a person as a result of getting smallpox.

a. _____

b. _____

10 Which statement is an opinion?

ⓐ Today, many people enjoy going to zombie movies and watching an imaginary virus spread all over the world.

ⓑ Smallpox is another deadly disease that killed many people.

ⓒ A plague known as the Black Death is an example of a pandemic that occurred during the Middle Ages.

ⓓ When Europeans first came to the New World, they brought the smallpox virus with them.

Time to Write!

Directions: Not all diseases are infectious diseases. With your teacher's help, choose a noninfectious disease from the list below, or with your teacher's permission, you may add a choice of your own. Research your topic using books or the Internet. Then write a short report explaining what you have learned about your topic. Use the back of the page if you need more space for writing.

celiac disease	diabetes	heart disease
fibromyalgia	narcolepsy	osteoporosis
Alzheimer's	schizophrenia	other: _____

Topic: _____

_____

_____

_____

_____

_____

_____

_____

_____

_____

_____

_____

_____

_____

_____

True Courage

The alarm went off inside the school. Margaret knew what the sound meant. The droning noise was a tornado alarm. The scheduled after-school jazz band practice had been over for nearly thirty minutes, but Margaret and four of her friends had begged Mr. Potts to stay for a little longer. They were so close to having their new piece of music mastered. Mr. Potts had agreed; he was excited by their enthusiasm. However, after a few minutes, they all had begun to notice the sky was getting dark, and the wind had suddenly picked up speed outside the school. Mr. Potts had left his phone on the desk in his office. He told the girls to follow him to his office, and they would check to see whether any weather alerts were being issued. As they walked to his office, the alarms had started going off.

Margaret had practiced the tornado drill just as many times as the other students, but she had an experience that she hoped none of the others had. She once survived a tornado that directly hit her old school when she and her family lived in Texas. She took only seconds to respond to the alarm.

Not even waiting for Mr. Potts to react, Margaret told everyone to move quickly to an interior room to the left. This room was where the choir usually practiced. Margaret knew there were no windows in that room. She and Mr. Potts then directed everyone to get into the tornado position so they would be safe from any debris that might fly through the air. Margaret joined Mr. Potts beside the other students. She kept encouraging everyone to not be afraid. She even talked about some fun things they had done that year in school. The alarm continued to blare, and the wind outside sounded ferocious, yet Margaret managed to encourage the other students, convincing them that everything would be fine.

When the alarm finally ended, Mr. Potts was able to check the local weather. A tornado had missed the school by less than half a mile. He then let the students call home to let everyone know they were okay. Mr. Potts told Margaret how proud he was of her and her quick thinking. "You knew exactly what to do, and you helped keep all the other students calm. You are a real hero, Margaret."

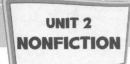
The Unsinkable Margaret Brown

In 1912, the *Titanic* was one of the most majestic cruise liners to ever sail on any ocean. The ship was called "unsinkable," and many of the rich and famous from all over the world were on board the ship when it set sail. One American passenger on board the ill-fated ship was Margaret Tobin Brown. Margaret was born in 1867 in Missouri. She was not raised with money, but she and her husband would later become extremely wealthy from mining silver. Even before she became rich, Margaret was an activist who fought for the rights of others. Later, she became a philanthropist and used her wealth to help those in need.

Margaret was sailing back home to America because she'd received word that her grandson was seriously ill. The ship promised to be the fastest transport to get her back home. Sadly, the return trip would be nothing like she imagined. Once the *Titanic* hit an iceberg at night and began to sink, women and children were urged to board the lifeboats. Margaret Brown helped take charge of the lifeboat she entered. She knew the panic among the passengers had to be stopped if they were to survive. The situation of those on board the *Titanic* was unthinkable as there were not enough lifeboats for all of the passengers. That night, Margaret became a hero.

On the night when the *Titanic* began to sink, she did what she could to help. She organized the survivors on board the lifeboat. She directed them all to steer toward the light of a ship she could see in the distance. This ship would later turn out to be the *Carpathia* and would rescue the survivors from the icy waters. Margaret realized that each person needed to take turns rowing the boat in order to stay warm. She'd also put on extra clothing when she left her stateroom. She shared the items she had and tried to help keep the other passengers from feeling the effects of the bitter cold.

Margaret would later be known in the newspapers by the nickname "Molly." She would eventually become famous as the "Unsinkable Molly Brown," even though she never called herself "Molly." What is true about Margaret Brown is her wish to help others and her ability to lead, no matter the circumstances.

The following pages have questions based on the texts from Unit 2. You may look at the stories to help answer any questions. Use the back of the page if you need extra space for writing your answers.

1 Why are Margaret and the other students staying after school?

   a They have band practice.

   b They have cheerleading practice.

   c They missed the bus.

   d They are helping Mr. Potts make posters for the pep rally.

2 Write the sentence(s) from the text that helped you to answer #1.

_____

_____

_____

_____

_____

3 What is one reason Margaret reacts quickly to the tornado alarm?

   a She does not like the loud noise.

   b She believes it is a fire alarm.

   c She experienced a tornado at her old school.

   d She was the only one who knew what to do.

4 What is one thing Margaret Brown does to help those on board the lifeboat?

   a She gives them all food and water.

   b She tells them which direction to row the boat.

   c She offers them all money.

   d She has coats for everyone on board.

5 Which word best describes each Margaret in both texts?

   a spontaneous

   b determined

   c reckless

   d fearful

6 Explain why the newspapers most likely began using the word *unsinkable* to describe Margaret Brown.

_____

_____

_____

7 In the text "True Courage," why does Margaret lead everyone into the choir room?

(a) She wanted to hear some music.

(b) She thought she heard voices coming from inside the room.

(c) She thought there would be food and water inside the choir room.

(d) She knew the choir room did not have any outside windows.

8 What does the word *philanthropist* mean as it is used in the following sentence?

Later, she became a philanthropist and used her wealth to help those in need.

_____

_____

_____

9 Based on what you know from the text, which statement is most likely true about Margaret Brown?

(a) She raised money to help the survivors from the *Titanic*.

(b) She immediately got on another ship and sailed back to England.

(c) She refused to ever speak to anyone about what happened on board the *Titanic*.

(d) She asked everyone to call her the "Unsinkable Molly Brown."

10 What do the two texts have in common?

_____

_____

_____

_____

Time to Write!

Directions: Think about what makes someone a hero. Then answer the questions below.

1. Using your own words, write a definition for the word *hero*.

   _____

   _____

2. Who is someone you know that you would call a hero? Explain why you believe this person is a hero.

   _____

   _____

3. Do you think you could ever be a hero? Explain your answer.

   _____

   _____

4. What is something you could do to help recognize or show appreciation for a hometown or local hero?

   _____

   _____

5. There are many fictional superheroes. What is the difference between a hero and a superhero?

   _____

   _____

6. If you could be a fictional superhero, what power would you want, and why would you want this super power?

   _____

   _____

   _____

Something Extra: On the back of the page, write a story in which you become the hero of the day!

Juliet looked carefully at her picture. She thought it was looking great. Her teacher would probably be very pleased with her work. She had only had to erase her lines one time, and she knew that after she finished coloring her picture, her mistake would no longer show.

"What type of homework are you doing?" Juliet's father asked. He walked past the table where Juliet was working and grabbed a bottle of water from the refrigerator.

Juliet looked up at him and answered, "It's a picture for school. Mrs. Camp, my art teacher, is working with my social studies teacher on a project for both classes. Tomorrow, we are going to begin studying something she called the 'arms race.' Mrs. Camp told us Mr. Mehaney would tell us more about it tomorrow in class, but she wanted us to draw a picture guessing what it might be. This is what I have drawn for her class."

Juliet's father came and stood behind his daughter and looked at the picture she had drawn.

"That's a great picture, Juliet. I would give you a good grade for your design and art work, but I think you definitely have a lot to learn about the topic."

"Mr. Mehaney said we could look up information after we drew our picture for Mrs. Camp. Maybe I should do that now."

"I'll help you," her father offered. For the next hour, they pored over articles they found on the Internet as Juliet read about the arms race. She learned the topic was about weapons or military arms after World War II; countries tried to make sure they had more weapons than other countries.

Juliet looked at her picture and laughed. She had drawn two human arms racing on their fingers. Both arms were trying to race to the finish line she had drawn and win a blue ribbon.

"I think my picture is pretty funny now," Juliet said. "I can't wait to show Mrs. Camp. I definitely have a lot to learn about the real arms race!"

World War II ended in 1945. The United States dropped the first atomic bombs ever used in history on the islands of Japan. Dropping the bombs ended the war in the Pacific. Japan surrendered after the second bomb was dropped on the city of Nagasaki. After four long years, World War II was finally over, but sadly, something new had started. The age of atomic bombs had begun.

The United States would soon find out it was not the only country that could produce an atomic bomb. By 1949, just four years after the United States dropped the two atomic bombs on Japan, the Soviet Union also had the capability to make an atomic bomb. A test bomb was dropped by the Soviets, proving the threat of nuclear power was no longer solely in the hands of Americans. Even though the two super powers had been allies during the war, the two countries were not on friendly terms. Each country wanted to be able to defend itself against the other. This rush to build military arms and have superior military strength became known as the "arms race." The United States and the Soviet Union each wanted to build bigger and better super bombs. The two countries also needed ways to release the bombs in case of attack. Each worked to have better missiles and airplanes to carry the bombs to their targets, if needed.

Eventually, both the Soviet Union and the United States would decide to negotiate so that neither country would use weapons of mass destruction. While John F. Kennedy was president of the United States, the two countries signed a treaty and agreed not to test any more nuclear weapons above ground. They also worked to open up easier communications between the two super powers. Nuclear energy is still part of our world today, but many countries work tirelessly to use this energy to help improve lives rather than destroy them.

The following pages have questions based on the texts from Unit 3. You may look at the stories to help answer any questions. Use the back of the page if you need extra space for writing your answers.

1 What do the two texts have in common?

(a) Both are about school projects.

(b) Both are about World War II.

(c) Both are about the arms race.

(d) Both are about an art contest.

2 What does the word *pored* mean as it is used in the following sentence?

For the next hour, they pored over articles they found on the Internet as Juliet read about the arms race.

(a) drizzled

(b) hid

(c) remained

(d) studied

3 Explain why the text is titled "A Different Meaning."

_____

_____

4 Which event began the arms race?

(a) dropping the atomic bombs on Japan

(b) being allies with the Soviet Union in World War II

(c) electing John F. Kennedy as the president

(d) making missiles to carry bombs

5 According to the text, which statement is a fact?

(a) Nuclear bombs should never be dropped.

(b) Nuclear energy is still a part of our world.

(c) Nuclear energy is the most cost-efficient energy available.

(d) Nuclear energy is no longer used by any country.

6 Explain what Juliet discovers after she does research with her father.

_____

_____

7 Use information from the text to explain why both the United States of America and the Soviet Union wanted to build up their supply of weapons.

_____

_____

_____

8 Why does Juliet believe her art teacher will be pleased with her work?

    ⓐ She understands the meaning of the arms race.

    ⓑ She has used unique colors in her picture.

    ⓒ She has done her best work in drawing her picture.

    ⓓ She is the only student who completed the assignment.

9 Which word is a synonym for the word *superior* as it is used in the following sentence?

This rush to build military arms and have superior military strength became known as the "arms race."

    ⓐ greater

    ⓑ weaker

    ⓒ multiple

    ⓓ singular

10 Explain why Mr. Mehaney might want his class to think about what they would be studying the next day.

_____

_____

_____

_____

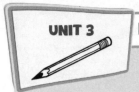

Time to Write!

Juliet is confused by the term "arms race," which is an idiom. Idioms are groups of words that can confuse people because they have a different meaning than the definitions to the actual words. For example, if someone tells an actor to "break a leg" right before he goes on stage, it does not really mean for him to break a leg. The person is wishing him good luck. If someone says it has "butterflies in his stomach," he actually means he is very nervous.

Directions: Use some of the idioms listed below, or research some of your own, and write a short story about a day you spent on a farm. Use the back of the page to complete your story. Remember to do the following:

- Use at least five idioms in your story.

- Circle any idioms you use.

at the drop of a hat	beat around the bush
can't judge a book by its cover	costs an arm and a leg
raining cats and dogs	chip on your shoulder
hit the nail on the head	piece of cake
taste of your own medicine	straight from the horse's mouth

Title: _____

_____

_____

_____

_____

_____

_____

_____

Something Extra: On a separate sheet of paper, list each idiom you used. Then explain the meaning of each idiom used in your story.

Precious Memories

Corinne sat on the floor beside a cardboard box filled with her things. Corinne's parents had brought up her belongings from the basement of their house. Feeling how damp the box was, she sighed out loud as she thought about the events of the past few days.

For almost a week, the sun had refused to shine. Instead, there had been nothing but clouds and rain in Corinne's hometown of Franklin. In fact, there had been so much rain that the creek outside of her family's home could not be contained in its banks. The creek water had poured over the banks, out into their backyard, and into the basement of their home. It had all happened so quickly that Corinne and her parents barely had time to move anything upstairs and away from the flooding basement. Corinne and her family were now spending the day trying to decide what could be salvaged from the flood. She was finally on the last box. It had been hard work throwing away some things that held such precious memories but were too ruined from the flood waters to think about keeping.

Her aunt came up with an idea that had at least made things a little easier. Corinne was thankful her aunt Lisa had come over to help them with the task. Not only had the extra set of hands been appreciated, but her ideas had been welcomed as well. She realized what a hard time Corinne was having because so many of her mementos could not be saved. Many items did not look ruined, but when someone touched them, they were saturated with water. Corinne's aunt had suggested they take pictures of each ruined item that was important to her. She said they could take all the pictures and put them in a scrapbook. Even though they would no longer have the item, they would still have the memory.

Everyone had agreed it was a great idea. The thought of making the scrapbook made cleaning out the basement more like a craft project and kept Corinne from being sad. Now, Corinne just wished her aunt would come up with a way to get the project done more quickly! Then everything would be nearly perfect.

Too Much of a Good Thing

Water is one of life's necessities. Without this precious source, life could not exist. However, too much of even a good thing can cause problems. Too much water can lead to flooding. When flooding occurs in areas that do not usually receive much water, anything living in the area is negatively affected.

Interestingly, not all flooding is bad. Some areas count on yearly floods to help the soil and to add water to areas that often face droughts, or lack of water. Yet when floods happen in areas that are populated by people, the results can be devastating to those who work or live in those areas. Many factors can cause flooding to occur. Heavy rains can be one cause. Another can be tsunamis or giant waves caused from typhoons or hurricanes that can cover entire cities with little advanced warning.

Flooding can also cause deadly results. In the United States, approximately 140 people die each year as a result of floods. On and near the continent of Asia, monsoon winds typically bring with them much needed rainfall to the area. However, in 1983, a monsoon brought with it torrential rainfall that was too much for the area to soak up. The flooding that followed caused massive damage to the country of Thailand. The monsoon winds were followed by deadly floods that caused many people to perish.

Flash floods are also dangerous. Flash flooding is generally a result of rain that comes down too fast for the ground or other water sources, such as creeks and rivers, to absorb. The result is flash flooding. Waters rise rapidly. Many motorists are caught unaware, especially at night when high waters are hard to see. They drive their cars on roads they normally travel, only to be swept away by quickly moving waters. Sadly, many people lose their lives as a result of flash flooding.

The following pages have questions based on the texts from Unit 4. You may look at the stories to help answer any questions. Use the back of the page if you need extra space for writing your answers.

1 Which word is an antonym for the word *precious* as it is used in the title of the text "Precious Memories"?

    (a) valued

    (b) treasured

    (c) prized

    (d) worthless

2 What do the two texts have in common?

    (a) Both are about flooding.

    (b) Both are about precious memories.

    (c) Both are about surviving a hurricane.

    (d) Both are about helping those in need.

3 Based on information from the text, which statement is true?

    (a) All flooding is bad.

    (b) Flooding can cause people to face many hardships.

    (c) No one has ever died as a result of flooding.

    (d) Floods are necessary for crops to grow in America.

4 What does the phrase "too much of a good thing" mean as it is used in the following sentence?

However, too much of even a good thing can cause problems.

_____

_____

5 Write the sentence(s) from the text "Too Much of a Good Thing" that best explain(s) how flooding can be a problem in the United States.

_____

_____

_____

6 List in chronological order three events that happened in the text "Precious Memories."

a. _____

b. _____

c. _____

7 Which paragraph in the text "Too Much of a Good Thing" best explains the dangers of flash flooding?

(a) paragraph 1

(b) paragraph 2

(c) paragraph 3

(d) paragraph 4

8 Write the sentence(s) from the text that best show(s) how Corinne feels about her aunt's idea.

_____

_____

_____

9 What does the word *negatively* mean as it is used in the following sentence?

Too much water can lead to flooding. When flooding occurs in areas that do not usually receive much water, anything living in the area is negatively affected.

(a) harmfully

(b) positively

(c) somewhat

(d) never

10 Explain how you chose your answer for #9.

_____

_____

_____

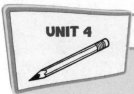

Time to Write!

Directions: Floods are not the only type of extreme weather problems that people have to face. Choose one of the extreme weather events listed below. Then write a short story in which you must survive the weather situation you have chosen. You may need to do some research about the extreme weather before you begin.

| hurricane | blizzard | tornado |
| lightning | heat | hail |

Title: _____

_____

_____

_____

_____

_____

_____

_____

_____

_____

_____

_____

_____

_____

Something Extra: On the back of the page, create an illustration for your story. Be sure to include a caption with your picture.

Just Watch

The sound of the ball caught Olivia's attention. She wondered who was already playing tennis on the court at the city park. She and her mother were usually the first ones to arrive each day. She rarely had any problem finding time to practice her favorite sport because the court stayed so empty. Olivia didn't understand why everyone didn't want to play tennis. Most of her friends played basketball or softball. A few were into soccer and volleyball. She was the only one who was passionate about tennis. She couldn't imagine her life without playing the game.

Olivia didn't recognize the two boys on the court. They were hitting the ball back and forth across the net. Olivia thought the two boys looked like they were about her age, but she'd never seen either of them at her school. She wondered whether they were part of a tennis team from a nearby neighborhood. Olivia's mother sat down on a park bench and pulled out her phone. She explained to Olivia that she planned to make a few phone calls while they were waiting for their turn to play. Olivia did not join her mother. She thought watching the other players would be more fun. She enjoyed watching tennis even if it was only a practice instead of a real game.

It didn't take long for the two boys to realize they had an audience. The boy to her right finally stopped the ball and held it. Then the two players walked over to the side of the court to speak to Olivia. Olivia found out the two boys were visiting their uncle who lived down the street from her. They played tennis at their school in Florida. One of the boys had hurt his wrist and was having a hard time playing. They asked Olivia if she'd like to take his place. She asked her mother for permission before agreeing to play. As they walked onto the court, the boy told Olivia he was sure he would beat her, but he would enjoy the practice. Olivia almost laughed when she realized he doubted she would be a very good player. Her hand tightened around her racket as she thought, *just watch*. After the ball went across the net, she met it with a firm hit from her racket. She watched the ball sail past her opponent before he even had time to react. Olivia was satisfied. She knew she had proven a point without saying a word.

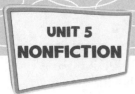
Women in Tennis

During the 1950s, Althea Gibson was known as one of the top female tennis players in the world. During this period in history, many people did not believe women could be strong competitors in athletic events. Amazing female athletes like Althea Gibson helped prove how wrong many of those people were.

Althea began playing paddle tennis, or tabletop tennis, when she was growing up in New York. People noticed her skills at the game and suggested she try playing tennis on a full court. She began training and became very good. She was so good, in fact, that she toured the world after she became a member of the United States national tennis team. Not only was Althea a breakout female athlete, she was also the first African-American female to play tennis at Wimbledon.

Another famous female tennis player was Billie Jean King. Billy Jean played tennis during the 1970s. She played during a decade when women did not always have equal rights with men. One inequality was in the amount of money women earned when they completed the same or equal task that men did. She was upset that men earned larger cash amounts in prizes than women did when competing at the same tournaments. This inequality caused Billie Jean King to react. She helped others who felt the same way as she did to establish a successful professional tennis tour for women.

Billie Jean didn't become a well-known name only because she wanted equality for women's pay in sports. She also became known for a tennis match where she played against a well-known male tennis player named Bobby Riggs. Everyone was anxious to see what would happen between these two players. The match was shown on television. She won the match and helped prove to many people all over the country and even the world that women could do just as well (if not better) than men at sports.

UNIT 5 QUESTIONS

Name

Date

The following pages have questions based on the texts from Unit 5. You may look at the stories to help answer any questions. Use the back of the page if you need extra space for writing your answers.

1 What does the word *opponent* mean as it is used in the following sentence?

She watched the ball sail past her opponent before he even had time to react.

- (a) someone who is your adversary
- (b) someone who is your ally
- (c) someone who is your friend
- (d) someone who is your neighbor

2 Write the sentence(s) from the text that show(s) how Olivia feels about playing tennis.

_____

_____

_____

_____

3 What do Billie Jean King and Althea Gibson have in common?

- (a) They both played tennis.
- (b) They both acted in movies.
- (c) They both sang the national anthem before a sporting event.
- (d) They both beat Bobby Riggs in a tennis match.

4 In the text "Just Watch," why are Olivia and her mother going to the park?

- (a) so Olivia can practice running for an upcoming marathon
- (b) so Olivia can meet up with some friends from school
- (c) so Olivia can collect leaves for her leaf collection
- (d) so Olivia can play tennis on the courts at the park

5 Explain why the text is titled "Just Watch."

_____

_____

_____

6 Why does Olivia play tennis with the boys?

    (a) One of the boys knows her.

    (b) She asks them whether she can play tennis.

    (c) One of the boys is hurt and can no longer play.

    (d) She demands that the boys share the tennis court.

7 What do the two texts have in common?

_____

_____

_____

_____

_____

8 List in chronological order three events that happened in the text "Just Watch."

    a. _____

    b. _____

    c. _____

9 List two adjectives that would describe both Billie Jean King and Olivia.

    a. _____

    b. _____

10 Think about the words you chose for #9, and explain why you chose the words you did.

    a. I chose the word _____ because _____

    _____.

    b. I chose the word _____ because _____

    _____.

Time to Write!

Directions: Many famous athletes endorse or help sell products. For example, you may see a famous athlete's name on a brand of shoe, or you might see his or her face on a box of cereal.

Choose a famous athlete or use one from the text you read, and design an advertisement for the breakfast cereal below. Draw a picture on the cover of the box. Be sure to include lots of strong adjectives describing the celebrity endorsement.

On the back of the page, write a paragraph explaining why you chose this particular athlete. Be sure to research the athlete you chose if you want to know more facts about him or her before you begin.

The morning was hot. The temperature was already in the eighties, and Dean knew the temperature was only going to get hotter. He also knew his grandfather needed his help, but he was not looking forward to working with no air conditioner all day while he helped his grandfather clean out his barn. His mother told him he would have fun, but when he felt the sweat start to gather on his face, he thought her idea of fun must be a lot different from his idea.

"Where should we start?" Dean asked his grandfather. He pointed Dean to the left side of the barn and explained that he would take the right side. He thought, between the two of them, they could finish the work in a couple of hours.

Dean began by shoveling out the straw scattered all over the floor of the barn. Next, he began straightening up his grandfather's tools, and then he started gathering other things to be put into the trash. He was beginning to feel very pleased with the work he'd done. The barn really was beginning to look a lot better, and with the easy conversation he and his grandfather had been having, the time had seemingly flown.

"Take a look at this, Dean," his grandfather's voice broke through his thoughts. "Come look at what I found. I completely forgot this was put out in the barn." His grandfather was holding a large radio. Dean recognized it from a picture that had been in his social studies book at school.

"It's an old radio!" Dean exclaimed. "I wonder if it still works?"

"Let's take it to the house and find out," his grandfather suggested. "My grandparents had one like this at their house when I was a boy. We used to sit around and listen to the radio like you watch and listen to the television today. The main difference is we'll have some of your grandmother's delicious lemonade while we do this, and that's a treat I bet you don't always get!"

In the 1930s, people gathered around with their families to listen to the radio as much as people today gather around the television to share and experience hours of entertainment. The radio became an important accessory in most homes. People listened for both news and entertainment from the stations that came through their radios. Music also became an even more popular form of entertainment than it already was, as people were able to hear a wider variety of styles. People could enjoy music from areas outside of their local regions. They were exposed to new and different types of music.

One particular radio show in 1938 caused quite a scare among many of those listening that night. The Mercury Theater Group presented a radio play that was an adaptation of a novel by H.G. Wells titled *The War of the Worlds*. The radio show was made to sound like a live news show. Like the novel, the radio play reported that Martians were invading Earth. Those who listened to the radio from the very beginning were aware that the invasion was fiction and that no aliens from outer space were landing on Earth. However, things were different for listeners who turned on their radios after the program had already started. Many of those listening that night were panicked, believing that Earth was being invaded by creatures from Mars. As word of the panic reached those performing live on the air, the radio show was temporarily interrupted, so the announcer could again remind the audience that what they were hearing was a fictitious story and not an actual invasion.

People would eventually lose their interest in radio dramas as television became the next best technology during the 1940s. People could both listen and watch with the new and improved invention. The first televisions were nothing like the technology we enjoy today. However, people were still enthralled with the idea of bringing both picture and voices into their homes and to be able to begin to see what they had only been able to imagine as they had listened to their radios.

UNIT 6 QUESTIONS

Name

Date

The following pages have questions based on the texts from Unit 6. You may look at the stories to help answer any questions. Use the back of the page if you need extra space for writing your answers.

1 Why does Dean begin to feel pleased with the work he has done?

(a) His grandfather praises him.

(b) His grandmother tells him he is doing a wonderful job.

(c) He uses his phone and takes a picture of the work he's completed.

(d) He sees how much work is getting done.

2 List two ways radios were important in homes during the 1930s.

a. _____

b. _____

3 During the 1940s, which invention replaced the radio in many American homes?

(a) computers

(b) cell phones

(c) televisions

(d) satellites

4 Explain why some radio listeners were quick to believe the United States had been invaded by aliens from Mars.

_____

_____

_____

_____

5 Which part of the text best helped you to answer #4?

(a) the title

(b) paragraph 1

(c) paragraph 2

(d) paragraph 3

6 Are people today ever fooled by radio or television programs? Explain your answer.

_____

_____

7 Why is Dean's grandfather excited about finding the radio?

   (a) He needed a new radio.

   (b) The barn is getting much cleaner.

   (c) The radio reminds him of a happy memory.

   (d) He thought some music would help make the work go faster.

8 List in chronological order three events that happened in the text "Voices of the Past."

   a. _____

      _____

   b. _____

      _____

   c. _____

      _____

9 What does the word *enthralled* mean as it is used in the following sentence?

People were still enthralled with the idea of bringing both picture and voices into their homes.

   (a) annoyed

   (b) fascinated

   (c) determined

   (d) uninterested

10 Write two facts from the text "From Radio to Television."

   a. _____

   b. _____

Time to Write!

Directions: In the Venn diagram below, compare and contrast modern radio to today's computers. Think about how they are alike and how they are different. List two ways they are unique and two ways they are the same. Label your diagram

Hint: Be sure to write the two ways they are the same in the section of the circles they share.

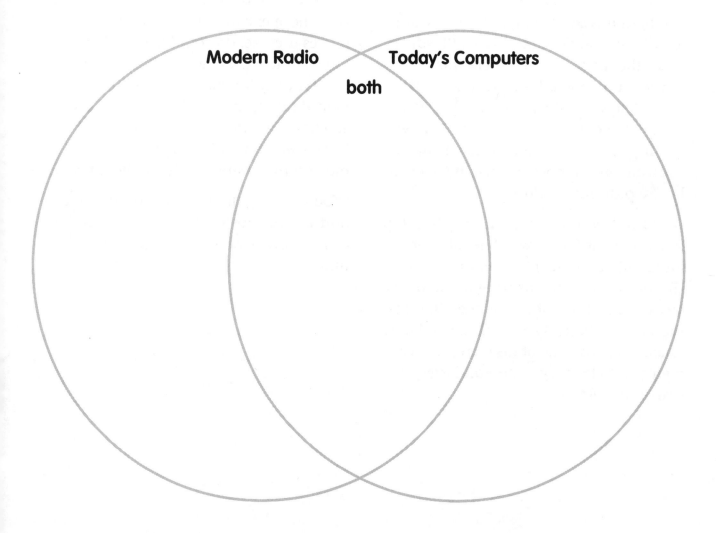

Something Extra: Think of another invention (from the past or from modern times), and compare and contrast it to today's computers or another invention of your choice. Write your answers on the back of the page.

Kayla couldn't believe two hours had passed so quickly. "Can't we go back in and watch the movie again?" she begged her mother as they exited the theater.

"Not today, Kayla. We're meeting your father for lunch," she gently reminded her.

"Well, that is something to look forward to at least," Kayla said, "but I still want to see the movie again. There was so much action and adventure, and you didn't know what was going to happen next. I hope they make a sequel." Kayla continued talking as they walked down the sidewalk and stopped outside the door to her favorite eating place.

At the restaurant, Kayla still couldn't stop talking about the movie. She told her father all about the plot and the main characters, but she was careful not to give away the ending. She explained that the president's plane, *Air Force One*, was being taken over, and one of his secret service men had to try to save him and everyone else on the plane.

"Just one?" her father teased.

"I wish I could grow up and be a hero," Kayla said.

"You know you can be anything you want to be, Kayla. You have your entire future ahead of you, but I don't think what happens in the movies is really what heroes are like, do you?" her mother asked. Kayla watched as her father stood up to pay for their lunch. She thought her father looked handsome in his police uniform. She knew her mother was right. Real heroes weren't make-believe characters in movies; they were people like her father.

"You're right, Mom, but I still want to go and see the movie again, and maybe our own family hero will go with me next time!"

Protecting the President

The president of the United States holds one of the most important offices in the world. Many people work to guard the president and keep him or her safe. The amount of protection surrounding the president has not always been as great as it is today. Not until the early 1900s, when an attempt was made on the life of President McKinley, did agents begin protecting the country's leader. Then in 1930, while President Hoover was in the White House, a stranger walked straight into the dining room where he was. Hoover then decided it was time for a change in protecting whoever was in office. He helped establish a special group to protect the president each day. As threats against the leader of the country have increased, so has the amount of security.

The Secret Service has the important job of protecting the leader of the United States. To keep the president safe, the Secret Service does many different things. One way they prevent others from causing harm is by keeping secret the exact information about where, when, and even how the president is planning to travel. This secrecy is just one step in making sure there are no problems.

Wherever the president does decide to travel, many security measures must be taken. Any place where the president might be on his or her travels is inspected for security. Even the president's food is inspected. Sometimes Secret Service agents must spend hours waiting on the president and keeping the area where he or she has traveled secured. Once they are positioned, they must watch for any suspicious situations that might be potential threats.

Of course, the men and women who are part of the Secret Service receive special training to do their jobs well. They are vital in making sure the president and those close by stay safe. Having such an important job is not always easy, but those who protect the president always know their job is important to not only the president but also the entire country.

The following pages have questions based on the texts from Unit 7. You may look at the stories to help answer any questions. Use the back of the page if you need extra space for writing your answers.

1 After reading the text "Protecting the President," what can one infer about the job of a Secret Service agent?

  (a) The job is exactly like it is shown in the movies.

  (b) An agent must spend some of the time waiting and watching.

  (c) A Secret Service agent receives little special training.

  (d) Well-trained Secret Service agents would need no special equipment to do their jobs.

2 What helps Kayla remember true heroes exist in real life?

  (a) seeing her father in his uniform

  (b) watching the action movie

  (c) talking to her mother about the movie

  (d) reading an article about a firefighter performing a dramatic rescue

3 According to the text, which two events caused a change in the way the president was guarded?

  (a) the assassination of President Kennedy and an attempted kidnapping of the president's child

  (b) President McKinley being shot and a stranger walking into the White House during President Hoover's time in office

  (c) an assassination attempt on the president's life and a threatening letter that was sent to the White House

  (d) a threatening letter that was sent to the White House and a rock being thrown at the president during a parade

4 What do the two texts have in common?

  _____

  _____

  _____

5 List two adjectives that best describe someone who is a hero.

  a. _____

  b. _____

6 Using information from the text, explain why the job of the Secret Service is important.

_____

_____

7 Compare the job of a Secret Service agent to the job of a police officer. List two ways they are alike and two ways they are different.

Alike

a. _____

b. _____

Different

a. _____

b. _____

8 What does the word *establish* mean as it is used in the following sentence?

He helped establish a special group to protect the president each day.

ⓐ continue

ⓑ finish

ⓒ begin

ⓓ learn

9 Write two facts from the text "Protecting the President."

a. _____

b. _____

10 The job of a Secret Service agent and a police officer can be dangerous. Explain why someone would choose to have a job in which they might be in danger.

_____

_____

_____

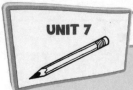
Time to Write!

Directions: Write an acrostic poem about heroes. Use the word *heroes* to help create your poem. Each line must begin with the letter that is given. Each line should be about your topic.

Hint: The lines of the poem do not have to rhyme.

> **Example**
>
> **Poem Title:** Everyday Heroes
>
> **H**elping people whenever they can
>
> **E**very person is a hero in his or her own way

Poem title: _____

H _____

E _____

R _____

O _____

E _____

S _____

Something Extra: On the back of the page, write a poem about a specific person you know who is a hero.

Samuel sat on his bed staring at the calendar on his wall. He couldn't believe it was time to go back to school; it seemed like winter break had just started. He didn't dislike fifth grade. His teacher was nice, and several of his friends were in his class, but he also liked being at home. Not having any homework was great, and he loved getting to sleep in each morning. His mother even had time to make him his favorite breakfast, pancakes, when they weren't rushing for him to catch the school bus.

"Why do you look so sad?" Samuel's mother asked. Samuel hadn't even heard his mother enter his room. "Are you a little worried about going back to school?" she asked. Samuel nodded, wondering how his mother always seemed to read his mind.

"You like school, don't you?" she gently questioned him. Samuel nodded again.

"I do, but I wish I didn't have to go tomorrow. I don't know why anyone made it a law that children have to go to school. We shouldn't have to go if we don't feel like going."

His mother sat down beside him on the bed. She put her arm around Samuel's shoulder. "You know, Samuel, I think you're right."

"You do?" Samuel couldn't believe what he was hearing. His mother, who was always going on about how important it was for him to get a good education, was saying he didn't have to go to school. This was incredible!

"Absolutely," she said. "Just make sure you get up an hour earlier than you normally do because it will take you all day long to complete the list of chores I'll have for you to do."

Samuel groaned. "What?" his mother looked at him innocently. "I said you didn't have to go."

"Just get me up at the normal time, Mom. You have a way of making me look forward to going back to school tomorrow!"

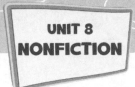

A Different Childhood

During the early 1900s, life was hard for many children of immigrants in the United States. Many people moved to America from other countries with the hope of having a better life for their families. When these immigrants arrived in America, they often found they had to work hard to survive in the "land of opportunity." Hard work did not involve just the adults in a family. Children often had to work if a family was to have enough money to afford food and shelter.

How were children supposed to help pay for what a family needed? During certain times in America's history, going to school was not mandatory. Children did not have to attend school. Many families wanted their children to go to school. They knew that getting an education would help them succeed in life, but there often was no time to let their children go to school. If their children were in school, then they weren't working. If they weren't working, then they weren't helping the family survive.

Because children could be hired to work, many employers wanted to hire them. Children did not have to be paid as much as adult workers, so this saved the companies money. So many children worked outside their homes that, by the 1900s, approximately 1.7 million children under the age of 15 were working in factories. Many of the factories that hired children made different types of clothes. Working around the machinery was perilous work, and many children got hurt working with such dangerous equipment.

Finally, things began to change in America. By 1918, children were required to attend elementary school. Working conditions also started to improve as stricter rules began to be enforced. Children had the chance to get an education and improve their way of life. The dream that had brought many of their families to America began to be realized as conditions slowly improved for all families. As a result of these changes, the "land of opportunity" was finally living up to its nickname.

UNIT 8 QUESTIONS

Name _____ **Date** _____

The following pages have questions based on the texts from Unit 8. You may look at the stories to help answer any questions. Use the back of the page if you need extra space for writing your answers.

1 Why is Samuel sad?

  (a) He can't find his homework.

  (b) He realizes winter break is over.

  (c) He doesn't want to do his chores.

  (d) He is having an argument with his mom.

2 How do you know Samuel's mother wants him to go to school?

_____

_____

_____

3 Why did parents in the early 1900s want their children to go to work?

  (a) They thought school was a waste of time.

  (b) They wanted their children to meet new people at work.

  (c) They liked having their children at work with them.

  (d) They needed the money their children would make to help the family survive.

4 Explain what the title "A Different Childhood" means.

_____

_____

_____

5 Using information from the text, explain how you can tell Samuel's mother cares about him.

_____

_____

_____

_____

6 What does the word *immigrants* mean as it is used in the following sentence?

When these immigrants arrived in America, they often found they had to work hard to survive in the "land of opportunity."

(a) people moving out of a country

(b) people moving across a country

(c) people moving into a country

(d) people moving into an apartment

7 What can you infer about life for immigrant children in the early 1900s?

(a) Life was very easy for immigrant children.

(b) Life was exactly the same as it is today for immigrant children.

(c) Life was often hard for immigrant children.

(d) Life was the same for immigrant children as it was for the children of wealthy Americans.

8 Which sentence best explains what the phrase "not mandatory" means as it is used in the following sentence?

During certain times in America's history, going to school was not mandatory.

(a) Children did not have to attend school.

(b) Children had the chance to get an education and improve their way of life.

(c) Children did not have to be paid as much as adult workers.

(d) Children often had to work if a family was to have enough money to afford food and shelter.

9 Write an adjective or phrase that would describe both Samuel and his mother.

_____

10 Give evidence from the text to support the answer you gave for #9.

_____

_____

_____

_____

Time to Write!

Use your powers of persuasion and try to get people to agree with your opinion. Use the back of the page if you need more space.

Part 1

Directions: Write a paragraph arguing why children your age should not have to attend school.

_____

_____

_____

_____

_____

_____

Part 2

Directions: Write a paragraph arguing why children your age should have to attend school.

_____

_____

_____

_____

_____

_____

_____

A Childhood Friend

Joanna tore off a piece of a tape and attached it to the side of the box. She had slowly been working on her room all day. Her family was moving to a new house, and her mother had put her in charge of packing her own room. She hadn't really minded. She simply hadn't realized there was so much to pack.

The floor of Joanna's bedroom was littered with boxes. On one side of the room, she had the things she wanted to move to the new house. On the other side of the room, she had the things she wanted to give to a charity. Joanna's grandfather knocked on her open door and then came into her room. She stood up from her seat on the floor and walked over to give him a big hug. She knew he understood how hard the move was for her. She could tell the move was hard on him, too. Joanna had lived across the street from her grandfather ever since she was born. She loved visiting him whenever she wanted. Her mother's new job was taking them two hours away. She and her mother had tried talking him into moving with them, but he hadn't decided yet what he would do. The house where he lived was the last one he had shared with her grandmother before she had passed away. It would be hard to leave a place filled with so many memories.

Joanna walked over to her bed and moved over a couple of items she'd placed there to make room so her grandfather could sit down. One of the items was a small teddy bear. He reached out and took it from her and held it between his hands. The fur on the bear was matted, and a small tear was on one of its paws. It was obvious that the toy had been played with and much loved. "So, Mr. Bear," Joanna's grandfather began talking to the stuffed animal, "it looks like you're going to move soon. I'd probably miss seeing your furry face, so don't tell Joanna yet, but it looks like I'll be moving soon, too! I just can't imagine not seeing this teddy bear every day." Joanna could not believe what she was hearing. Everything would be okay if her grandfather was coming, too. Suddenly, she was in a much bigger hurry to get everything packed.

The History of the Teddy Bear

A lot of people have a beloved toy from their childhood. This toy may be special because of the person who gave the toy or because of the memories from playing with the object. If you asked several people what their favorite childhood toy was, you should not be surprised to find that, for many of these people, their special toy was a teddy bear. People of all ages still have these soft, stuffed bears. They come in all shapes and sizes. No matter what they look like, you will hear most people refer to these cuddly creatures as teddy bears.

So where did the name "teddy bear" come from? Why is the word *teddy* placed in front of the word *bear*? The answer is an interesting story that involves the twenty-sixth president of the United States, Theodore Roosevelt, who also went by the nickname Teddy.

Roosevelt was an avid outdoorsman. He enjoyed spending his time hunting, and he went on hunting trips whenever he could. It was a particular hunting trip in 1902 that would forever link the twenty-sixth president with the stuffed animal that would later become known by his name.

Roosevelt was invited by the governor of Mississippi to participate in a hunting trip for bear. After three days of hunting, many in the party had spotted a bear, but the president had not. Those who had headed up the trip were worried about this, so they let dogs loose to track a bear and then tied the injured animal to a tree for the president to hunt. Roosevelt felt this was not sportsmanlike, and he would not shoot the bear. Political cartoonists heard the story and drew pictures of Roosevelt refusing to shoot the bear. Eventually, the bear in the cartoons became smaller as new ones were drawn, and the bear in the picture became the size of a cub. A toy maker, whose wife sewed stuffed bears, had an idea. He asked for President Roosevelt's permission to call the toy a "teddy bear," and the rest is history!

The following pages have questions based on the texts from Unit 9. You may look at the stories to help answer any questions. Use the back of the page if you need extra space for writing your answers.

1 Why does Joanna most likely not mind packing up the things in her room?

- (a) She can make decisions about what to keep.
- (b) She does not trust anyone else to do the job.
- (c) She wants to hide some things in the boxes that her mother told her not to pack.
- (d) She does not want to help pack the rest of the house.

2 What might be one reason why Joanna's grandfather pretends to talk to her teddy bear to deliver his important news?

- (a) because there are many happy memories connected with the toy
- (b) because he is extremely shy
- (c) because he wants Joanna to give him the bear
- (d) because he is trying to make Joanna sad

3 What famous person in history is associated with the teddy bear?

_____

4 Why did the president refuse to shoot the bear?

- (a) He had already finished hunting.
- (b) He thought it would not be fair to kill a bear that was restrained.
- (c) He only wanted to hunt for deer.
- (d) He did not enjoy hunting.

5 Based on what you have read in the texts, write a word that would describe both Joanna and President Roosevelt. Explain your choice.

Word: _____

Reason: _____

_____

_____

6 Why does Joanna believe her grandfather is not going to move?

    (a) He cannot leave his current job.

    (b) He does not want to move where Joanna is moving.

    (c) He does not believe Joanna's mother wants him to move.

    (d) He will not want to move away from the house where he had lived with his wife before she passed away.

7 How did news of the story of President Roosevelt and his hunting trip most likely reach other people?

    (a) through the Internet

    (b) through word of mouth

    (c) through the radio

    (d) through newspapers and magazines

8 Which sentence(s) from the text helped you to answer #7?

_____

_____

_____

_____

9 The text "The History of the Teddy Bear" states that "eventually the bear in the cartoons became smaller as new ones were drawn, and the bear in the picture became the size of a cub." Explain why this most likely happened.

_____

_____

_____

10 Write two facts from the text "The History of the Teddy Bear."

    a. _____

    b. _____

Time to Write!

Directions: Imagine you are a toy inventor. Create a stuffed animal that you want named after someone famous. Then create an advertisement that will be heard only on the radio and will promote your new idea. Be sure to do the following:

• Draw and color your creation in the space below. Use the picture to help you think of words to describe your new toy and to write your advertisement.

• Write an advertisement that will both explain and promote your new stuffed animal.

• Be clear about why the animal is being named after the famous person you have chosen.

• Include where your product can be purchased.

Fire!

Mason was dreaming about a cookout. He and his friends were sitting around a fire and cooking s'mores. He loved the way the chocolate melted onto the cracker once he added the hot marshmallow. He wanted to cook the fluffy, white treat exactly right. He liked it to be golden brown but never burnt. His marshmallow was almost perfect when suddenly it burst into flames. No matter how hard he tried, he couldn't stop it from burning. He could smell the smoke. He watched as all his friends backed away from the fire, and then he jerked away from the flames, and suddenly he was awake. He sat up in his bed thinking that had to be one of the strangest dreams he had ever had. It had all seemed so real. It was almost as though he could still smell the fire burning. Mason took a deep breath to help clear his thoughts. When he did, he smelled smoke.

He realized with a start that he really was smelling smoke. This was not a part of his dream. Something in his house was on fire! Mason jumped up from his bed. His bedroom door was open. He looked down the hall. There was no smoke or flames. His parents' bedroom was across the hall. He ran straight into their room and woke them up. He quickly told them about his dream and waking up to the smell of a fire. His father ran down the hall to find the source. His mother grabbed her phone to call for help when they heard him yell, "It's okay. I know where the smell is coming from. Everything is okay. Come see for yourselves."

Mason and his mother went down the hall and found Mason's father in his office. He was standing beside his desk that was right next to a window. The window was wide open. "I opened this window earlier to get some fresh air from outside. I'm sorry, but I guess I forgot to close it. The wind is blowing in the direction of our house, and the smoke blew this way."

Mason realized the smell was even stronger now. He and his mother walked over to the window and looked out before closing it. Their next-door neighbors had a small outdoor fire going, and it looked like several people were still gathered around cooking s'mores. "That explains it," Mason said to his family. "I guess maybe that also explains why I was dreaming about s'mores!"

Most animals are born with several senses that they use to help them survive. Animals' senses vary depending on which one they need. One sense that is strong in some animals is the sense of smell. Of course, people are born with the sense of smell. We can smell both good and bad smells. A person can smell food that makes him hungry, or a person can smell something bad and know to avoid whatever is making the horrible scent. However, as good as people's noses are, they are nothing compared to the ability some other animals have. Their sense of smell is often used daily to help them survive.

The ability to smell is part of an animal's olfactory system. This system works to varying degrees in different species. Sharks, for example, have an amazing sense of smell. A shark can separate the smell of blood from all the other smells in the water. The shark can use the smell as a trail to follow to find its victim. Sharks aren't the only animals that have such an awesome ability.

A Gila monster is another animal with a great sense of smell; however, the Gila monster performs this task a little differently than other animals. This particular animal doesn't use a nose to gather scents. It uses another part of its body: its tongue! The Gila monster uses its forked tongue to gather scents. It flicks its tongue in and out of its mouth to help it pick up smells. The tongue can be used to gather both smells from the air and those on the ground. When the tongue touches anything, the scent is immediately sent to the Gila monster's brain where it processes the information and knows whether it has found something to eat or not.

Obviously, all animals are not alike. The ability to smell, however, is often important for survival. People are lucky to have this as one of their major senses. People can use the ability to smell to help them find good things and avoid unpleasant situations or disasters.

The following pages have questions based on the texts from Unit 10. You may look at the stories to help answer any questions. Use the back of the page if you need extra space for writing your answers.

1 What do the two texts have in common?

    (a) Both are about the sense of sight.

    (b) Both are about the sense of taste.

    (c) Both are about the sense of touch.

    (d) Both are about the sense of smell.

2 Explain why Mason believes something in his house is on fire.

_____

_____

_____

3 What other sense besides the sense of smell does Mason use to help figure out what is actually happening? Use an example from the text to support your answer.

_____

_____

_____

_____

4 What is unusual about the Gila monster's sense of smell?

    (a) The Gila monster uses its eyes.

    (b) The Gila monster uses its ears.

    (c) The Gila monster uses its tongue.

    (d) The Gila monster uses the pads of its feet.

5 According to the text, why did Mason most likely wake up in the middle of the night?

_____

_____

_____

6 Based on information from the text, what can you infer about the shark's sense of smell?

(a) The sense of smell helps the shark find food that it needs to survive.

(b) The sense of smell helps the shark avoid things in the ocean that smell bad.

(c) The sense of smell helps the shark find places to rest.

(d) The sense of smell helps the shark find other sharks.

7 Why did Mason most likely dream about cooking s'mores on a campfire?

(a) He went to bed hungry.

(b) He could smell the neighbor's campfire.

(c) He wanted to go camping.

(d) He dreamed about s'mores every night.

8 Why is it important for a shark to be able to identify the smell of blood?

(a) It helps the shark find hurt animals in the ocean.

(b) It helps the shark avoid other animals.

(c) It helps the shark find its way back home.

(d) It helps the shark camouflage itself from predators.

9 What would be another adjective that could replace the word *amazing* in the title "Amazing Sense of Smell"?

_____

10 Explain why you chose the word you did for #9.

_____

_____

_____

_____

Time to Write!

Directions: With help from your teacher, research an animal that has an amazing sense of sight. Decide on an animal to research. List five facts about the animal. Make sure some of the facts are about its amazing ability to see. Then write a short report about what you have learned. Use the back of the page if you need more space.

My animal is a(n) _____.

Five Facts

1. _____

2. _____

3. _____

4. _____

5. _____

My Report

_____

_____

_____

_____

_____

_____

_____

_____

_____

_____

_____

Night Hike

Five girls gathered with their troop leader at the start of a narrow trail. The girls were going on a night hike. All of the girls except Paige had been on a night hike before. The troop of experienced hikers was going to help Paige earn a special badge for completing the hike in the dark. It was dangerous for anyone to do on their own. Unlike day hikes, night hikes make it hard to see where you are going. The troop could not go without an adult, so they were glad when Mrs. Brewster had agreed to take them. Paige welcomed the company. She was excited to earn her badge.

"Is everyone ready?" Mrs. Brewster asked the girls. Everyone agreed they were ready. The group started off down the trail. As they walked, the girls were quiet. They were listening for sounds in the dark. It did not take long for them to hear an owl. Its distinctive hooting let them know the birds of night were starting to become active. Along the trail, the group would stop and look for tracks of animals using the light of the full moon to help them see. Paige was excited when she recognized the prints of deer in the soft mud that ran along the edge of the trail.

"Well, Paige," Mrs. Brewster said, "you've heard the sound of a bird at night, and you've spotted animal tracks on our hike, but there is at least one more thing you need to find. You need to discover flowers that bloom at night."

Paige was puzzled. She didn't know that any flowers bloomed at night. She thought flowers only bloomed during the day. She told Mrs. Brewster what she thought.

One of the girls in the troop spoke before Mrs. Brewster could answer. "That's what I thought, too, Paige. Imagine how surprised I was when I went on my first night hike. I learned there are all kinds of flowers that wait until night to bloom. They use animals such as moths and bats to help spread their pollen." Paige couldn't wait to find her first night flower. She decided this would be the first of many group night hikes for her.

In the Night

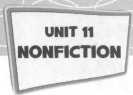

Daytime is not the only time flowers bloom and animals are busy. Nighttime is also an exciting time for nature and all its activities. Animals that are nocturnal are active during the night hours rather than during the day. There are also plants that are active at night. Some even bloom by the light of the moon instead of the sun!

Most people know that bats are nocturnal animals. But did you know that bats can help spread pollen? Bats are attracted to the smells that certain plants produce. These night-blooming plants need animals or insects to spread their pollen just like plants that bloom in the day. Bats drink the nectar from certain flowers. As they drink, pollen from the flowers fall onto the bats. The bat takes this pollen with it when it flies away and spreads it to other flowers much as bees do during the day.

Some plants, like evening primrose, open up and bloom after the sun is gone from the sky. Flowers that bloom at night are usually white or pale so they appear to glow in the dark. Moths at night act in much the same way as butterflies do in the day. As a moth flies from flower to flower to drink, pollination occurs. This means the flower will be able to grow seeds, and new flowers will be created.

Night animals receive food from the plants and flowers they visit. Plants are able to spread pollen and create more plants, thanks to their nightly visitors. Plants that bloom in the night and nocturnal animals both need each other. This partnership between the two is called *mutualism*. Both benefit from each other. As daylight comes, different animals and different plants become part of nature's spotlight, but one should never forget that nighttime is host to a spectacular nature show all on its own.

The following pages have questions based on the texts from Unit 11. You may look at the stories to help answer any questions. Use the back of the page if you need extra space for writing your answers.

1 According to the text "Night Hike," what is one reason a night hike might be more dangerous than a hike during the day?

(a) It is impossible to call for help if it is needed.

(b) It is harder to see at night.

(c) It is too easy for people to get tired.

(d) It is the time dangerous animals are out in the woods.

2 Paige thinks the night hike will be the first of many group night hikes for her because

(a) she does not think she will earn her badge.

(b) she likes being with her new friends.

(c) she is enjoying the night hike.

(d) she thinks the members of her troop will make her go again.

3 Write a sentence from the text "In the Night" that defines the word *nocturnal.*

_____

_____

_____

4 What do the two texts have in common?

(a) Both are about hiking at night.

(b) Both are about plants and animals that are active at night.

(c) Both are about endangered animals.

(d) Both are about the cycles of the moon.

5 Which sentence is an opinion?

(a) Daytime is not the only time flowers bloom and animals are busy.

(b) Nighttime is also an exciting time for nature and all its activities.

(c) Animals that are nocturnal are active during the night hours rather than during the day.

(d) There are also plants that are active at night.

6 Why were the girls quiet as they began the hike?

(a) They were not allowed to talk during the hike.

(b) They were listening for the sounds of nighttime animals.

(c) They all were listening to music through their headphones.

(d) They were upset and did not want to talk to each other.

7 According to the text, what is *mutualism*?

(a) a situation in which each partner receives a benefit from the arrangement

(b) a situation in which neither partner benefits from the arrangement

(c) a situation in which one of the two partners benefits from the arrangement

(d) a situation in which only someone or something connected to the partners receives any benefits

8 Explain why flowers that bloom at night are usually light-colored or white.

_____

_____

_____

_____

9 List two night creatures from the text "In the Night" that help plants to pollinate.

a. _____

b. _____

10 Which paragraph from the text "In the Night" best explains the important job of moths that fly at night?

(a) paragraph 1

(b) paragraph 2

(c) paragraph 3

(d) paragraph 4

Time to Write!

Directions: Use the space below and the back of the page if needed, and write a short play about an adventure that happens in the woods at night. One of the main characters must be a bat. You can add at least three more characters to your play. Be sure to include dialogue between the characters.

Hint: Begin a new line each time a different character speaks.

Example

Bat: I have a terrible problem.

Mole: What is it, bat?

Bat: I am scared of the dark.

Play Title: _____

_____

_____

_____

_____

_____

_____

_____

_____

_____

_____

_____

_____

The Nesting Place

Kristen's foot slipped on the rocks. She reached out and grabbed a nearby branch to stop her from falling.

"Are you okay?" Kristen could hear the concern in her little sister's voice. Kristen was quick to assure her that she was fine. It was the second time that day she'd almost fallen. The trail they were on was covered with loose rock and pebbles. Kristen wished she had worn her hiking boots instead of her tennis shoes, but it was too late now to worry about things she hadn't done. If what her father said was true, she knew they were almost there. Just a few more feet, and they would be able to see an eagle's nest.

"Dad said we could see the nest once we rounded the next bend on the trail. At least we remembered to bring the binoculars," Kristen said.

Allison held up the binoculars and offered them to Kristen. "You can use them first."

"No, you go first," Kristen said. "You carried them the entire way. It's only fair that you look before I do." The two girls reached the spot where their father had told them to go.

Allison raised the binoculars to her eyes and then whispered, "I see it, Kristen. I see the nest." She handed the binoculars to Kristen so she could look, too. Kristen looked at the large nest and then brought the binoculars away from her eyes. At that moment, both girls saw a huge shadow go over the rocks just in front of them. The shadow had enormous wings. They looked up and saw a beautiful sight. A bald eagle was flying back to the nest. The water from the Cumberland River was below the nest. They watched as the eagle made a dive toward the river and then came back up with a fish captured between its large talons.

The two stayed for a while longer and watched. Then they began their hike back down the trail. When they reached the bottom of the trail, Kristen said, "I can't believe I forgot to take a picture."

"I don't think we need a picture," Allison told Kristen. "I think that is something both of us will never forget!" Kristen thought about the giant shadow and how majestic the eagle had looked, and she knew her little sister was right.

Eagle Pride

The bald eagle is one of the United States's most recognized symbols. On June 20, 1782, the bald eagle was officially chosen as a symbol for the country. The majestic bird appears on the Great Seal of the United States. It can also be found on many types of money. The eagle is recognized as America's national bird. The bald eagle is the bird that is most associated with the United States, but there are, in fact, many other types of eagles. Eagles can be found on every continent in the world except for Antarctica, where the extreme temperatures prohibit many animals from existing.

Not all eagles grow to be as large as the bald eagle. One eagle in Australia is quite small. From wingtip to wingtip, it only measures about three feet. The same eagle only weighs a little more than a pound. In contrast, the largest eagle is a harpy eagle from South America. This eagle can weigh as much as twenty pounds. The female of this species is larger than the male, which is usually only about half as large as the female bird. A bald eagle is neither large nor small. An average bald eagle weighs about nine pounds. Despite the wide width of its wings, this eagle usually weighs less than the average house cat! Small or large, eagles have at least one trait in common. They are excellent predators. They rely on catching fish, mammals, and sometimes even other birds for their diet. Eagles usually carry their prey to their nests. Dining high above the ground is much safer for these birds.

If our nation's symbol is to survive in the wild, people must learn to live in harmony with the eagle. They must be willing to protect the forestlands where eagles build their nests. People must also be careful when using certain chemicals and poisons. These can harm both the eagles and their unhatched eggs. Many people have worked hard to help keep and maintain the habitats eagles need to survive. As their population increases, don't be surprised if you look in the sky one day and see a beautiful eagle flying overhead.

The following pages have questions based on the texts from Unit 12. You may look at the stories to help answer any questions. Use the back of the page if you need extra space for writing your answers.

1 Why are Kristen and Allison hiking?

   (a) They want to get some exercise.

   (b) They want to see a bald eagle's nest.

   (c) They want to take pictures of the eagle's nest for their school newspaper.

   (d) They want to surprise their parents by telling them they found a bald eagle's nest.

2 Write one or two sentences from the text that proves Kristen and Allison have a good relationship as sisters.

_____

_____

_____

_____

_____

_____

3 What do the two texts have in common?

_____

_____

_____

4 Which statement is not true about eagles?

   (a) They are predators.

   (b) They come in many different sizes.

   (c) They are extinct.

   (d) They do not like to eat their food on the ground.

5 What is another symbol that represents the United States other than the bald eagle?

_____

6 What does the phrase "live in harmony" mean as it is used in the following sentence?

People must learn to live in harmony with the eagle.

_____

_____

_____

7 According to the text, what are two things that have the symbol of the eagle as part of their design?

a. _____

b. _____

8 What is one reason why a bald eagle might make its nest near a river?

_____

_____

_____

9 Which sentence(s) from the text helped you to answer #8?

_____

_____

_____

10 What is the purpose of a symbol or emblem?

ⓐ to represent something

ⓑ to explain something

ⓒ to understand something

ⓓ to ignore something

Time to Write!

Directions: The bald eagle is a symbol that represents the United States of America. Many schools also have mascots that are symbols that represent their schools. Imagine you are opening a brand-new school in your town. You are in charge of choosing an animal to be a symbol for your new school. Answer the questions below to help explain your choice.

My new school will be represented by the following animal: _____

There are two main reasons I chose this animal to be our school's mascot. The reasons are as follows:

a. _____

b. _____

One thing people might not know about this animal is _____

_____.

Two words that best describe this animal are _____ and _____.

Some people might think this is a bad choice for our school's symbol because . . .

_____

_____.

This isn't true because _____

_____.

Everyone should be able to agree that this animal is the perfect choice to represent our

new school because _____

_____.

The British Are Coming!

James adjusted his coat and looked one last time in the mirror. He was satisfied with the way the costume looked. He was amazed at what his mother could do with a needle and thread. Most of his friends' mothers couldn't sew. For his mother, sewing was something she had learned to do as a little girl. James remembered her trying to teach him to sew when he was little. He could sew on a button and do a few simple stitches, but he had never picked up the skill the way his mother had. When he needed a costume to play the part of Paul Revere in his school play, he knew his mother would know what to make.

"You look wonderful in your costume."

James turned around and saw his mother standing in the doorway to his room. "Thanks to you," he said before walking over and giving her a hug.

"You're going to be a wonderful Paul Revere," his mother added. "I think you had the hard part of getting ready for this play. You had all those lines to memorize. Making your costume was a snap compared to what you had to do."

"Do you know what my favorite line is from the entire play?" James asked.

"What?"

"Really, Mom? You can't guess?" She smiled as understanding hit her, and at the same time, she and James hollered out, "The British are coming!"

James's mother straightened up his coat and handed him his hat as she scooted him out the door. "You, young man, had better move it because, if we're late, there won't be anyone to warn those poor people about the British, and who knows what will happen then!" James just shook his head at his mother's humor, but he quickened his pace as they headed out the door.

Paul Revere

Paul Revere lived in the colony of Massachusetts in the town of Boston. Paul Revere was part of the Sons of Liberty. This group met to discuss the colonists' grievances against the British king, King George III, who ruled over the thirteen American colonies. The original thirteen colonies were located along the Eastern coast of what is now the United States. There were many different reasons the colonists were unhappy with British rule. However, many of those reasons revolved around taxes the colonists felt were unfair.

During the French and Indian War, Paul Revere had fought on the side of the British. As the years passed, Revere began to believe, as many others did, that the colonies were not being treated fairly by Great Britain. This atmosphere of animosity between the colonists and the British soldiers erupted in gunfire on March 5, 1770. Colonists began throwing snowballs and rocks at British soldiers. In the confusion, one soldier thought he heard his captain yell to begin firing on the unarmed colonists. Five colonists were dead before the shooting stopped.

More British soldiers poured into the colonies to help get things under control. Revere and the other Sons of Liberty acted as spies, listening for important information. Revere believed the British would march on Concord because the colonists were storing war supplies there. To prepare the colonists for such an invasion, Revere knew he needed a system to warn everyone if the British were coming. There were two routes the British could take to reach Concord. One route was by land, and the other was by sea. He set up a light in a tall steeple to signal the colonists. A single light would mean the British were coming by land. Two lights would mean the British were coming by sea. Revere and two other men, William Dawes and Samuel Prescott, would also ride by horse to warn everyone about the soldiers' arrival. Contrary to popular belief, Paul Revere did not ride through the streets shouting that the British were coming. This would have given away the secrecy of his mission. Regardless, his famous ride has become a favorite part of America's history.

The following pages have questions based on the texts from Unit 13. You may look at the stories to help answer any questions. Use the back of the page if you need extra space for writing your answers.

1 What can you infer about James's relationship with his mother?

(a) They do not get along very well.

(b) They are very close to each other.

(c) They rarely speak to each other.

(d) They have little interest in what each other does.

2 During what time period is the setting of James's school play?

(a) after the Civil War

(b) after the French and Indian War

(c) during World War II

(d) during the time of the dinosaurs

3 Which would be a good alternative title for the text "Paul Revere"?

(a) "Against All Taxes"

(b) "An American Patriot"

(c) "Freedom Isn't Free"

(d) "The French and Indian War"

4 What does the phrase "quickened his pace" mean as it is used in the following sentence?

He quickened his pace as they headed out the door.

_____

_____

_____

5 Why did Paul Revere no longer support British rule?

(a) He felt the British were treating the colonists unfairly.

(b) He met the king and did not like him.

(c) He thought the thirteen colonies should be ruled by France.

(d) He wanted to become the president of the thirteen colonies.

6 Why were the British planning to march on the city of Concord?

    (a) They believed the colonists were storing war supplies in Concord.

    (b) They believed several spies were hiding in Concord.

    (c) They believed the people who lived in Concord owed taxes to the king.

    (d) They believed the king was being held captive in Concord.

7 What does the word *grievances* mean as it is used in paragraph 1 of the text "Paul Revere"?

    (a) complaints

    (b) compliments

    (c) promises

    (d) advice

8 What do the two texts have in common?

    (a) the thirteen colonies

    (b) the Revolutionary War

    (c) Paul Revere

    (d) King George III

9 Which sentence from the text best explains how James feels about his mother's ability to sew so well?

_____

_____

_____

_____

10 What would a single light mean to the colonists who saw it?

    (a) The British were no longer coming.

    (b) The British were coming by sea.

    (c) The British were coming by land.

    (d) The British were coming by air.

Time to Write!

Part 1

Directions: Imagine you could travel back in time and interview Paul Revere. Think of four questions you would ask Paul Revere if you had the chance to talk to him. Write your questions below.

1. _____

2. _____

3. _____

4. _____

Part 2

Directions: Choose one question from Part 1. With your teacher's help, use the Internet or books from the library to find the answer to your interview question. Based on what you can infer he would say, write Paul Revere's answer in the space below.

Question # _____

Paul Revere's answer:

_____

_____

_____

_____

_____

_____

_____

_____

_____

So far, Mark's morning had not gone well. He'd overslept even after his mother had told him it was time to get up. He'd barely had time to get dressed when he heard his sister yelling that the bus was coming. Grabbing his backpack and running out the door had left him no time for breakfast. He wasn't sleepy anymore, but he was definitely hungry. His stomach growled loudly, and several of his classmates sitting close to him laughed. Even the teacher, Mr. Samuels, seemed to have heard. He looked up from his notes and straight at Mark before continuing his lecture. Mark shifted uncomfortably in his seat, wishing the class could go quicker. His lunch period was next, and he couldn't wait to eat.

"Early civilizations were often built on the edges of rivers," Mr. Samuels' voice broke into Mark's thoughts of food. "Living near a river could be both a curse and a blessing. Floodwaters could rise quickly and cause great damage to the cities built near the rivers. Those same waters could also help keep the soil fertile and allow crops to flourish and grow." Mr. Samuels paused to see whether his students were taking notes. Then he looked around the room before asking the class a question. "Can anyone give me any other reasons why living near a river might have been a blessing?"

"Transportation would be easier if an ancient city was built near water," one student said.

"People who lived in the cities would have a constant source of water they could use," another student added.

"Those are all great answers," Mr. Samuels said. "Mark, do you have any ideas you could add to what has already been said?"

All eyes in the classroom turned to look at Mark. At that exact same moment, Mark's stomach let out a loud growl that everyone in the room could hear. Mark knew he should be embarrassed, but instead, he was relieved because his hungry stomach had given him the perfect answer to Mr. Samuels' question. "My answer is food, Mr. Samuels. Living near a river would provide ancient civilizations with a quick and easy source for food." Everyone laughed as the bell rang, and Mark rushed out of the room to find his own close source of food.

Ancient Waters

The ancient land known as Mesopotamia was located between two rivers, the Tigris and the Euphrates. The land between these two rivers would also become known as the Cradle of Civilization or the Fertile Crescent. The two rivers allowed civilization in this area to flourish. Where is this ancient land? It was located in what is known today as the southern portion of Iraq. Even today, the two rivers play an important role for the cities that have developed near them.

For a civilization to grow and thrive, there must be a reliable source of water. Rivers give a continuous source of water. A land with two rivers has an abundance of resources for any civilization hoping to continue to expand. Yet, the land between the Tigris and Euphrates Rivers was not the only ancient area to rely on a river source for its water. Ancient Egypt was another area that counted on a river to sustain life. Even today, the Nile River provides much needed water in an area that is mainly a desert region. The soil near the banks of the Nile provided an abundance of plants for both humans and animals. Like many rivers, the Nile could also cause problems when the waters overflowed the banks. Too much flooding could wash away fields of crops. Not enough flooding could lead to drought and poor harvests. The ancient Egyptians relied heavily on the waters of the Nile.

Where there is water, there is also an abundance of wildlife. Not only do fish inhabit the waters of the rivers, but ducks and other water fowl make their homes near the river. These animals helped provide another source of food for the people who lived near them.

Today, rivers are often controlled by manmade systems. These systems help manage flooding, which might otherwise be a problem. Due to improvements in transportation and technology, people are no longer forced to build their cities and homes near rivers. Yet, these ancient sources of water played an important part in the history of civilizations, and they will continue to play a major role in modern times and for generations to come.

UNIT 14 QUESTIONS

Name _____ **Date** _____

The following pages have questions based on the texts from Unit 14. You may look at the stories to help answer any questions. Use the back of the page if you need extra space for writing your answers.

1 Why is Mark having a difficult time concentrating at school?

    (a) He missed the bus, and he is upset.

    (b) He forgot to do his homework, and he is going to be in trouble.

    (c) He did not eat any breakfast, and he is hungry.

    (d) He is sleepy, and he cannot focus on what the teacher is saying.

2 Based on information from the texts, give two reasons why early civilizations would have been built near a source of water.

    a. _____

    _____

    b. _____

    _____

3 Why was the land between the Tigris and the Euphrates Rivers called the Fertile Crescent?

    (a) The crescent-shaped land had a large enough water source that living things could grow and flourish.

    (b) The land between the rivers was shaped in the form of a crescent.

    (c) The area of land received large amounts of rainfall each year.

    (d) The words *Fertile Crescent* are easier to pronounce than the names of the rivers.

4 Explain why cities of today are not always built near a major source of water.

_____

_____

_____

5 What happens that helps Mark answer Mr. Samuels' question?

    (a) He remembers seeing the answer in his notes.

    (b) His friend whispers the answer to him.

    (c) Mr. Samuels' gives him a hint.

    (d) His stomach growls.

6 List two examples that show why Mark is having a bad day.

a. _____

b. _____

7 What does the word *abundance* mean as it is used in the following sentence?

A land with two rivers has an abundance of resources for any civilization hoping to continue to expand.

(a) more than enough

(b) not enough

(c) an exact amount

(d) a small portion

8 In the text "Ancient Waters," which paragraph best explains the importance of the Nile River?

(a) paragraph 1

(b) paragraph 2

(c) paragraph 3

(d) paragraph 4

9 What do the two texts have in common?

_____

_____

_____

_____

10 Mark's stomach is growling in class, and he is embarrassed. Should Mark be embarrassed by this? Explain your answer.

_____

_____

_____

Time to Write!

Directions: With help from your teacher, research and learn about the Amazon River, the longest river in South America. Use the Internet or other book sources to find five facts about this amazing stretch of river. Be ready to share your facts with other students in your class.

The Amazon River

Fact 1: _____

_____

Fact 2: _____

_____

Fact 3: _____

_____

Fact 4: _____

_____

Fact 5: _____

_____

Something Extra: On the back of the page, write a story about you and a friend exploring the Amazon River. Be sure to use some of the facts you have discovered when writing your adventure.

No Money for Fun

Max shook his piggy bank, but nothing else came out. Scattered on the floor all around where he was sitting were several different coins. He turned the piggy bank back around and put his eye up to the hole to look inside. "Is it totally empty?" a voice from behind Max spoke up. Max put down the piggy bank and turned around to talk to his older brother, Chad. Chad knew Max was counting all of his money, and he knew how much he wanted to buy a new game that was coming out next week. Chad was the one who had suggested he count all of his change. Until he'd mentioned it, Max had forgotten about the piggy bank in his room.

Max showed Chad the empty bank. "I think I have about half the money now, but I don't know where I'm going to get the other half. It's horrible being broke," Max complained.

Chad laughed and patted his brother's shoulder. "Max, you don't know what it's like to be really broke. You just don't have enough money to buy something you want. You don't need the game. There's a big difference."

"Maybe," Max said, "but I still feel like I'm broke."

Chad snapped his fingers as an idea hit him. "I think I know how you can get the money you need, Max." Max waited for his brother to share the rest of his idea. Max knew Chad always had great ideas. If anyone could help him, it would be his big brother. "What if we split the cost of the game?" Chad suggested. "I could pay for half, and you could pay for half, but that would mean I would get to play with it just as much as you do." Max couldn't believe his luck. His brother was the best. He nodded his head vigorously as he agreed, and then he shook his brother's hand.

"That's the best idea I've ever heard," Max said. "I'll even let you play first."

Chad interrupted Max before he could say anything else. "I don't think I like that idea."

"You don't?" Max was confused. He thought Chad would want to go first. "No, I don't," Chad said. "I think once we get it, we should both play it together." Max grinned; his brother really did have the most amazing ideas.

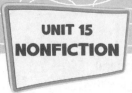

Hard Times

The 1930s brought hard times for many Americans. The economy began to struggle as less spending occurred. The decade of the 1920s had been a time of increased spending for many citizens. As World War I ended, people were glad to have life settle back into normal routines. People began to spend money on new luxuries, such as washing machines and radios. People used a system of spending where they would buy large items using credit. This means they would pay for an item over several payments rather than paying all at once for a purchase. Eventually, people's spending habits began to slow down. They already owned many of the items they'd rushed to buy only a few years earlier. This lack of spending hurt many businesses. This also caused a decline in jobs because production slowed down. Through a series of events that all hurt the economy, America went into a time called the Great Depression.

During the Great Depression, many people lost their jobs. Unable to work, many people also lost their homes. Even finding enough food to eat was a problem for many families. Soup kitchens opened to help feed those who were hungry. People in the cities would wait in line for long periods of time to try to receive food to eat. Volunteer workers helped serve these meals to those who needed them. Many people were forced to live wherever they could. Those who lost their homes would use cardboard boxes or pieces of wood to try to make some type of shelter. Because the people felt the government was doing little to help, they blamed President Hoover for the horrible economy. Americans began to refer to the homeless areas where people lived as Hoovervilles. Franklin D. Roosevelt would eventually become president. He promised to help the country out of the Depression by offering a program that came to be known as the New Deal. He worked with the government to help create jobs to help those who wanted to work. People who lived during the hard times of the 1930s were thankful for President Roosevelt's leadership. Eventually, America became embroiled in World War II. The Great Depression finally came to an end, but those who lived through the decade never forgot the lessons learned from living through hard times.

The following pages have questions based on the texts from Unit 15. You may look at the stories to help answer any questions. Use the back of the page if you need extra space for writing your answers.

1 Why is Max counting his money?

   (a) He wants to buy a new game.

   (b) He wants to give his brother some of his money.

   (c) He wants to take his money to the bank.

   (d) He wants to find a special penny he has lost.

2 What can you infer about Max's relationship with Chad?

   (a) They do not get along.

   (b) They get along very well.

   (c) They seldom talk to each other.

   (d) They do not have anything in common with each other.

3 What do the two texts have in common?

_____

_____

_____

_____

4 Write the sentence(s) from the text "Hard Times" that explain(s) what it means to purchase something using credit.

_____

_____

_____

5 Which sentence is not a fact?

   (a) During the Great Depression, many people lost their jobs.

   (b) As World War I ended, people were glad to have life settle back into normal routines.

   (c) Soup kitchens opened to help feed those who were hungry.

   (d) America managed not to get involved in World War II.

6 Explain why Chad offers to help Max pay for the new game.

_____

_____

7 Which would be a good alternative title for the text "Hard Times"?

    (a) "Something for Everyone"

    (b) "A Time to Play"

    (c) "A Great Hope"

    (d) "America's Decade of Depression"

8 Explain why you chose the answer you did for #7.

_____

_____

_____

_____

9 Explain why buying on credit might not always be a good idea.

_____

_____

_____

_____

10 What was the nickname given to the cardboard cities built during the Great Depression?

    (a) Roosevelt Towns

    (b) Hoovervilles

    (c) Depression Homes

    (d) Sad Cities

Time to Write!

Directions: During the Great Depression, many people needed help. Some people helped by finding jobs for those who needed them. Others helped give food to the hungry. Some helped make clothes. There were many ways that people worked together to help those in need. Imagine you had $100. Think about what you could do with that money to help someone else. Use the questions below to help decide what you would do with the money you have.

Hints: If you want to mention a classmate's name, be sure to get his or her permission first. Also remember, you can't keep the money for yourself.

1. I would want to help _____.

2. I chose this person/people to help because _____

_____

_____.

3. The $100 could be used to _____

_____

_____.

4. The reason this would be helpful is because _____

_____

_____.

5. If someone asked me why I wanted to spend the $100 this way, I would just explain

to them that _____

_____

_____.

The Ring

Heather and her father were walking on the beach. Her father was helping her collect shells. Each morning of their vacation, she and her father would set an alarm to get up early. Her older sister thought she was crazy to set an alarm while they were on vacation, but Heather loved seeing the sun rise each day. Getting up so early also meant there were more shells to look at on the beach. Heather was gathering shells that looked special to her. Then she would take pictures of them to put in the scrapbook she was making of their vacation.

"What about this one?" Heather's father asked her as he picked up a shell from the sand. Heather saw all the swirls of purple and white on the covering of the shell. It was beautiful and in perfect shape. She took a picture before her father placed it back on the sand.

"I think I see something," Heather said as she walked a few steps forward and then dug her fingers in the wet sand. "Dad, I've found something, and it's not a shell!" Heather held up her discovery so her father could see.

"Why, it's a wedding ring," he said, taking the gold ring from her fingers. He brushed off the sand and then turned the ring so he could look at the inside of the band. "There's an engraving here with a name. It says 'Janice Matthews, I'll love you forever.'"

Heather took a picture of the ring and then her father handed it back to her as she slipped it in the pocket of her shorts. "I think we should try to find who this belongs to, Dad."

"I agree," he said. "The ring is made of gold, so it is worth money, but a ring like that is worth more than gold."

"What do you mean?" Heather asked.

"A wedding ring is circular because it is a symbol of a love that has no end just as a circle never ends. I bet whoever lost this will be very happy if we can find them." Heather knew it would be hard to find the owner, but she agreed with her father. The gold was valuable, but the meaning of the ring was worth so much more.

Gold

Gold has been an important metal for thousands of years. Gold is remarkably strong and can be shaped into many forms, yet it will not break. Because gold was considered valuable in ancient cultures, having gold meant having wealth. Along with that wealth, people who owned gold were often very powerful. Rulers of countries and empires wanted to amass as much gold as they could. They sent explorers into faraway lands to help acquire fortunes for their kingdoms.

Ancient Romans used a gold band as an engagement ring. This tradition of wearing a gold band has been passed down to modern times. A gold band is often a symbol of marriage. However, people do not simply wear gold as rings. Many other pieces of jewelry are made from the precious metal. In ancient times, people also used gold for things such as crowns, bracelets, and pendants.

Two other ancient civilizations known for their use of gold were the Aztecs and the Incas. The Aztec empire was located in Mexico and existed somewhere around the 1400s and early 1500s. The people in this civilization believed that only certain people should be allowed to wear gold because it was such a precious metal. The Aztecs had a strong belief system in their gods. Because they believed the gods were important, they made crowns of gold for their statues. The Incan people also lived in Mexico around the same time as the Aztec civilization. This ancient culture believed only royalty should have access to gold. They believed their emperor was related to the sun god, so they used gold to build beautiful temples to honor both the god and the emperor.

Gold is still important today. Many people own gold jewelry that they wear daily or for special occasions. People also still mine for gold, although their systems are much more sophisticated than they were thousands of years ago. Based on the world's history with this unique metal, gold will remain an important product to the world.

UNIT 16 QUESTIONS

Name

Date

The following pages have questions based on the texts from Unit 16. You may look at the stories to help answer any questions. Use the back of the page if you need extra space for writing your answers.

1 Which character trait is true about Heather?

(a) She is selfish.

(b) She is boring.

(c) She is selfless.

(d) She is stingy.

2 Based on evidence from the text, explain your answer choice for #1.

_____

_____

_____

_____

3 Which is not true about gold?

(a) Gold can be used to make jewelry.

(b) All money is made from gold.

(c) Some ancient cultures made golden crowns for their gods.

(d) People today still mine for gold.

4 Which part of the text "Gold" best explains how the Aztecs used gold in their ancient culture?

(a) paragraph 1

(b) paragraph 2

(c) paragraph 3

(d) paragraph 4

5 What does Heather's father mean when he says, "a ring like that is worth more than gold"?

_____

_____

_____

6 Based on what the reader knows about Heather, why does she most likely take pictures of the shells and then place the shells back in the sand?

    (a) The shells are too fragile and will break if she carries them.

    (b) Heather wants to leave the shells there for other people to enjoy.

    (c) She does not want to get sand all over her.

    (d) She doesn't really like the shells.

7 What did a gold band represent to the ancient Romans?

    (a) three wishes

    (b) a marriage promise (or engagement)

    (c) wealth and happiness

    (d) good fortune

8 List two reasons why people might still mine for gold.

    a. _____

    _____

    b. _____

    _____

9 How might Heather and her father try to find the owner of the gold ring they found on the beach?

    _____

    _____

10 Which word is a synonym for the word *amass* as it is used in the following sentence?

Rulers of countries and empires wanted to amass as much gold as they could.

    (a) lose

    (b) gather

    (c) sell

    (d) build

Time to Write!

Directions: The idioms below use the word *gold*. Write the meaning of each idiom on the lines. Remember, an idiom is a group of words that has a different meaning than the definition of each individual word.

> **Example**
>
> It's raining cats and dogs: It is raining extremely hard, or there is a lot of rain.

1. All that glitters is not gold: _____

_____

_____

2. Good as gold: _____

_____

_____

3. Have a heart of gold: _____

_____

_____

5. Worth your weight in gold: _____

_____

_____

6. The golden years: _____

_____

_____

Patty stood back and looked carefully at the scene before her. The lighting was not quite right. She looked up at the sky, waiting for the cloud to move. She looked back through the lens of her camera. *Snap!* She took the picture. She knew it would be perfect.

Carefully gathering up her equipment, she thought about all the pictures she had taken during the week. Being at her grandparents' house had given her so many new things to photograph. She loved her home with her parents in the city, but it was wonderful to come to the country where there were so many different animals and plants.

Patty walked up the gravel road that led to her grandparents' house. She was pleased to see her grandmother sitting out on the porch in her favorite rocking chair. Patty knew she wanted to capture the moment in time by taking a picture. She quickly unpacked her camera and focused in on her subject. She snapped several pictures before her grandmother saw her.

"Oh, Patty, I know you could find something better to take pictures of than me." She smiled at her granddaughter as Patty joined her on the porch.

"I think these pictures are going to be my favorite of all the ones I've taken while I've been here," Patty said as she leaned over to give her grandmother a kiss on the cheek. "But do you want to know what my most favorite pictures of all are?"

"Which pictures, Patty?"

"The ones I keep in my mind of each trip I spend with you and grandfather. No matter where I am or what I am doing, I can always pull out those pictures and look at them again and again and remember how much I love being here with you both."

Dorothea Lange

The Great Depression was hard for people living in America. During the 1930s, many people could not find work, lost their homes, and even had a hard time getting enough food to eat. One photographer helped capture what was happening to the American people. Dorothea Lange's images taken during the Depression helped express what many people were unable to do in words. The expression that "a picture is worth a thousand words" has never been truer than in the photographs taken by Dorothea Lange.

Dorothea was born in 1895. Although her parents divorced when she was ten, both of her parents wanted her to have a good education. When Dorothea graduated from high school, she decided to learn all she could about photography.

As hard times began to hit America, Dorothea captured the moments with her camera. She began taking pictures of what she saw happening around her, including breadlines where people stood to try to receive free meals. She also snapped pictures of people going on labor strikes to try to get better working conditions. Dorothea and her husband would soon begin traveling the country, documenting the hard times people in rural areas were experiencing. Her husband wrote about what they saw, and Dorothea took pictures of what they encountered.

One of Dorothea's best known photographs is a picture called "Migrant Mother." The picture shows the emotions and hardships faced by a mother and her children as they struggle to survive during the Great Depression. Eventually, Dorothea's pictures would appear in various newspapers and magazines. The images she captured with her camera helped everyone in the country to see how farmers and their families were suffering as a result of the drought and hard economic times so many Americans were facing. Once people saw the picture "Migrant Mother," food was sent within days to those people who were in need of help. The expressions and emotions Dorothea captured in her photographs were worth a thousand words.

The following pages have questions based on the texts from Unit 17. You may look at the stories to help answer any questions. Use the back of the page if you need extra space for writing your answers.

1 What do the two texts have in common?

(a) photography

(b) the Great Depression

(c) family

(d) farming

2 How did Dorothea Lange's pictures help those suffering in the Great Depression?

(a) People were offered jobs.

(b) People were able to move to other countries.

(c) People were given food.

(d) People were given new homes.

3 Which paragraph in the text "Dorothea Lange" best explains why Dorothea was taking pictures of the people during the Great Depression?

(a) paragraph 1

(b) paragraph 2

(c) paragraph 3

(d) paragraph 4

4 Which pictures does Patty tell her grandmother are her favorite pictures?

_____

_____

_____

5 Explain why Patty says those pictures are her favorite.

_____

_____

_____

6 What do Patty and Dorothea have in common?

_____

_____

_____

7 Explain the meaning behind the expression "a picture is worth a thousand words."

_____

_____

_____

8 Based on what you know from the text, how would Patty most likely feel about the expression in #7?

(a) She would not agree with the expression.

(b) She would not understand the expression.

(c) She would agree with the expression.

(d) She would have no opinion about the expression.

9 Write an opinion statement about the text "Dorothea Lange."

_____

_____

_____

10 Based on information from the text, what can you conclude about Dorothea Lange's importance in helping others understand the hardships people faced during the Great Depression?

_____

_____

_____

Time to Write!

Directions: With your teacher's help, research a picture taken by Dorothea Lange or another picture from a different, well-known photographer. Use the space below to write about the image. Describe the photograph so that anyone who has not seen the picture would be able to imagine it simply from the words you have written.

_____

_____

_____

_____

_____

_____

_____

_____

_____

_____

_____

_____

_____

_____

_____

_____

_____

_____

An Unusual Surprise

The boat seemed to slide effortlessly out into the deep waters. Addie and her brother, Jackson, both watched the water lapping against the boat as they stood out on the deck. Their mother was sitting near them in one of the many deck chairs. Addie knew her mother wasn't as excited as she and Jackson were about the trip. She had grown up near the ocean and had been out on boat trips many times. She was the one who had suggested they go today. Addie thought there was something her mother wasn't telling them. She noticed every so often her mother would look at both her and Jackson and then smile like she had a secret.

Both Addie and Jackson seemed to notice at the same time that the boat was slowing down. Before they could ask, their mother walked over and joined them by the rail and explained, "The captain is stopping the boat here to let the passengers see something special." Addie knew then that she had been right. Her mother had been keeping a secret. She had known all along the boat would stop. She wondered what they would see. Maybe there would be a dolphin or a sea turtle in the water since they were so far out from the shore.

All of a sudden, Addie saw a dark form underneath the water. Then it looked like the water was parting. She grabbed her brother's arm, and they both took a step back in surprise as a large form came straight out of the water and up into the air before splashing back into the water.

Both Addie and Jackson screamed at the same time, "That was a whale!"

"I wish you could have seen the looks on your faces," their mother said. "Oh, but wait, you can. I just took a video." She held up her camera to show them she really had.

"Mom, this is amazing!" Addie said as another whale jumped out of the water and splashed back down into the sea. Jackson agreed with Addie. Then all three of them leaned against the rail and enjoyed the nature show.

Incredible Whales

Whales are incredible mammals, although many people think they are fish. They have lungs and need to breathe air the same as people do. Whales are also classified as mammals because they are warm-blooded, and their babies are born alive rather than hatched from eggs. An interesting fact that many people may not know is that male whales are called bulls, and female whales are called cows. So, what do you think a baby whale is called? A baby whale is called a calf!

There are two categories of whales. They are divided into whales that have teeth and whales that do not, or baleen whales. Baleen whales have brushes instead of teeth. Baleen whales are much bigger than whales with teeth. Part of this reason is most likely because of the way the two different types of whales get their food. Baleen whales eat plankton and do not need to hunt. They do not have to be fast as they go through the water getting food. On the other hand, whales with teeth must catch their food. Their somewhat smaller size helps them chase their prey. In fact, killer whales are such great hunters that groups of these whales have even attacked and killed other whales! Another difference between the two types of whales is their coloring. The bodies of whales with teeth are usually darker on top. These whales are much lighter underneath. This unusual shading helps camouflage the large predators from other animals in the water.

Sadly, many whales have been hunted, so several types are close to extinction. People hunted the whales as a source of oil and as a source of food. Today, people realize there are other options besides killing whales for food and oil. These changes, along with efforts from organizations working to protect the whales, have aided in helping whales remain an integral part of the world's oceans.

The following pages have questions based on the texts from Unit 18. You may look at the stories to help answer any questions. Use the back of the page if you need extra space for writing your answers.

1 How did Addie and Jackson feel about their mother's surprise?

(a) upset

(b) excited

(c) nervous

(d) afraid

2 If Addie and Jackson's mother told them she had another surprise for them, how would they most likely react?

(a) They would not want to know what the surprise was.

(b) They would refuse to see the surprise.

(c) They would never want to be surprised again.

(d) They would want to see the surprise.

3 Using information from the text, explain why you chose the answer you did for #2.

_____

_____

_____

_____

4 According to the text, what is one reason some whales are close to extinction?

(a) They have lost their habitat.

(b) They have lost their food source.

(c) They have been hunted.

(d) They are having fewer calves.

5 What does the word *extinction* mean as it is used in #4?

_____

_____

_____

6   Which statement is not a fact?

     (a) Whales are incredible animals.

     (b) Whales are mammals.

     (c) Male whales are called bulls.

     (d) Baleen whales have brushes instead of teeth.

7   Explain why the answer you chose for #6 is an opinion and not a fact.

_____

_____

_____

_____

8   Which would be a good alternative title for the text "An Unusual Surprise"?

     (a) "A Day in the Sun"

     (b) "Hiking Adventures"

     (c) "Whale Watching"

     (d) "Something for Everyone"

9   Based on evidence from the text, what is one reason whales with teeth are smaller than baleen whales?

_____

_____

_____

10   Explain why Addie thinks her mother has a secret.

_____

_____

_____

_____

Time to Write!

Part 1

Directions: Everyone knows whales are giant creatures of the sea. Find synonyms for the word *giant*. List six words that could be used to describe the size of these amazing ocean mammals.

1. _____

2. _____

3. _____

4. _____

5. _____

6. _____

Part 2

Directions: Choose at least four of the six synonyms you wrote in Part 1. Use the words in a story about whales. Circle the words you use.

_____

_____

_____

_____

_____

_____

_____

_____

_____

_____

_____

Midnight Snack

The noises in the night seemed loud to Carole as she crept downstairs to get a midnight snack. Each step she took seemed to creak. The sound of the icemaker was loud as the frozen cubes fell from the tray. Carole did not want to wake up her mother. She knew her mother had worked an extra shift at the hospital, and she was tired. Carole had made her mother a tray of food and taken it to her room, but she had already fallen asleep by the time she carried it up to her. Carole had put a piece of chocolate cake on the tray for her mother. She couldn't help but think how good a piece of that cake would taste with a glass of cold milk. She just didn't want to wake up her mother as she attempted to grab her snack.

Carole breathed a sigh of relief when she finally made it to the kitchen. Standing in the middle of the room, she decided not to turn on the light. Instead, she would use the light from the refrigerator to help her see. She opened the door and pulled out the gallon of milk and then poured herself a large glass. She grabbed a tray from on top of the refrigerator and then put the tray on the counter before adding the glass of milk. After she put away the milk, she took the top cover off the cake plate and then cut herself a large slice of cake. She placed this on the tray before shutting the refrigerator and grabbing her tray. She couldn't believe she'd woken up so hungry, but she planned to take her midnight snack straight to her room.

The hall seemed dark after the light from the refrigerator. Carole was turning the corner to head up to her room when she saw someone coming down the hall. She recognized who it was immediately. "Mom! Did I wake you up?" Carole asked her mother.

"You didn't wake me," her mother said, "but your brother came in earlier to tell me good night and told me I missed out on some chocolate cake you tried to bring me. I kept dreaming about chocolate frosting, so I decided to make my dreams come true."

"I think I've got just what you need," Carole said, following her mother to the kitchen for a special midnight snack.

Our Changing Sleep

Long ago, artificial light was not a part of people's lives. Once the day turned into night, without electric lights, the world they lived in became extremely dark. In some cases, that darkness also meant that it was dangerous to be outside. Who knew what might be lurking in the dark, waiting and watching? Because of the lack of light, people who lived long before you did the only logical thing they could do. They went to sleep.

Today's world has made our natural sleep patterns different than they were so many years ago. People's lives are no longer dictated by the hours the sun is out or the number of hours of darkness that nature provides. In fact, most people are constantly surrounded by some type of light source. Modern inventions, such as televisions and cellular phones, often put out light even when the lights are turned off. In some larger cities, there is so much artificial light that when there is a blackout of electricity and the city is thrown into darkness, people do not even recognize what they see in the night sky. For example, in 1994, there was an earthquake in Los Angeles that caused the city to lose its artificial light. During the event, the police department received several similar calls from different residents in the city. These calls were to report a strange, silvery-looking cloud in the sky above the city. What was this strange shape hovering over Los Angeles during the dark hours of the night? It was the Milky Way galaxy, which is always in the night sky.

No one will deny the importance of Thomas Edison's invention of the lightbulb. Whether the addition of artificial light into the lives of mankind is always a good thing is up to each person to decide. Maybe if everyone could learn to turn off the lights and get enough sleep each night, then there would be no debate. One thing is certain: The sleeping patterns of humans were forever changed by the invention and increasing use of artificial light.

UNIT 19 QUESTIONS

Name _____ **Date** _____

The following pages have questions based on the texts from Unit 19. You may look at the stories to help answer any questions. Use the back of the page if you need extra space for writing your answers.

1 Which statement is true about Carole's character?

   ⓐ She is selfish and doesn't want to help others.

   ⓑ She never wakes up during the night once she goes to sleep.

   ⓒ She is scared of the dark.

   ⓓ She cares about the people in her family.

2 Based on evidence from the text, explain your answer choice for #1.

   _____

   _____

   _____

   _____

3 What do the words *artificial light* mean as they are used in the following sentence?

Long ago, artificial light was not a part of people's lives.

   ⓐ light that is real

   ⓑ light that is not from a natural source

   ⓒ light that only comes from a flashlight

   ⓓ light that only occurs once it is dark outside

4 List one way Carole uses artificial light during the night.

   _____

   _____

5 According to the text, why did several people call the police during a blackout in 1994 after an earthquake occurred in Los Angeles, California?

   ⓐ They needed to leave the city.

   ⓑ They reported a strange cloud in the sky.

   ⓒ They wanted to know when the electricity would come back on.

   ⓓ They asked for the police to help find their missing pets.

6 Why is Carole being so careful to not wake her mother?

(a) Her mother has worked two shifts and needs to get some sleep.

(b) Her mother has a big meeting the next day.

(c) Her mother has a bad headache and needs to get some sleep.

(d) Her mother has asked that no one in the family disturb her.

7 At the end of the story, why does Carole tell her mother she has just what she needs?

(a) She has a room ready where her mother can go and get plenty of sleep.

(b) She can get her mother a piece of chocolate cake.

(c) She has some earplugs her mother can use while she is sleeping.

(d) She can get her mother some extra blankets for her bed.

8 Using evidence from the text, list two reasons why people's sleeping patterns were changed by the invention of artificial light.

a. _____

_____

b. _____

_____

9 Based on the text, give one reason why artificial light is not always a good addition to people's lives.

_____

_____

10 Which word choice could best replace the word *dictated* in the following sentence?

People's lives are no longer dictated by the hours the sun is out or the number of hours of darkness that nature provides.

(a) changed

(b) ruled

(c) endangered

(d) focused

Time to Write!

Directions: Many people like to tell spooky tales when it gets dark outside. Use the space below to write your own spook-tacular story to be told in the dark!

Today was the big day. The place where Danny and his family lived hosted a neighborhood yard sale each summer. Cars filled with people would show up from all over town to come to the sale. People seemed to love parking their cars and walking from house to house in search of the best deal or finding the perfect treasure to take home with them. Danny also loved the yard sale but not for the same reason that everyone else did. Danny had found his own way to make money during the annual event.

Three years ago, Danny had been helping his mom run their family's sale when he noticed that several of the people shopping looked hot and a little tired. He heard many people complain about the heat. He also heard some customers saying they needed something to drink. From watching and listening, Danny had an idea for the next sale. With his mother's permission, Danny set up a small outdoor covering. It was the same one his family used to cover their picnic table whenever they went camping. Next, he set out several lawn chairs in the newly made shade. Finally, he set up a small area where he posted a sign that let people know he had lemonade for sale. With his new idea and a few supplies, Danny was in business and ready to start making some money of his own.

It didn't take long for the customers to start flocking to Danny's area. Many of them wanted to sit for a minute and enjoy the shade. All of them wanted an ice-cold glass of lemonade. By the end of the first day, Danny had made more money from his lemonade stand than he did from an entire week of selling his items at his mother's yard sale.

Danny hopped out of bed ready to begin selling his lemonade for this year's sale. He liked that his mother told everyone how proud she was of him and that he was her own little entrepreneur. He was proud, too, that he had started his own business. He couldn't wait until his mother saw the new ideas he had added for this year's sale. He felt sure everyone, including his mother, would love the changes he had made.

A Little Ingenuity

A little ingenuity, or having clever ideas, goes a long way when trying to find a way to make money. This is especially true for anyone who is young enough to still be in school. For many young people, finding a job that will help them earn some cash is hard to do. Age and transportation to and from a place of employment can both be deterrents for young people hoping to find a way to make some money. However, there are some ways younger people can earn money.

One great way for younger people to earn that extra money to buy things or to save is to become an entrepreneur and become their own boss. How can you make this happen? Think about the area where you live. Create your own job by thinking of something that needs to be done in your area that you could do. If you live in a subdivision with a lot of pets, maybe you could open a pet-sitting service. Is there a way to recycle all the cans people in your area don't recycle? Maybe you could start a business that helps the environment and you at the same time! Finding a need is the best first step in finding a way to start your own business and make money.

Another important part of starting a business is knowing what you should charge your customers. If you charge too much, you probably won't have a lot of repeat business. If you don't charge enough, you may not be able to cover your expenses or make any money. One way to decide how much you should charge is to check with other similar businesses and see what they are charging. You can probably find out most of this information by using the Internet to search similar services. Once you feel like you have the information you need, set your price, and then decide the best way to advertise what you are going to do. Getting the word out to your customers is necessary if you want to be successful. Running your own business is not easy; however, if done well, it can be both rewarding and profitable.

UNIT 20 QUESTIONS

Name _____ **Date** _____

The following pages have questions based on the texts from Unit 20. You may look at the stories to help answer any questions. Use the back of the page if you need extra space for writing your answers.

1 What do the two texts have in common?

_____

_____

_____

2 From what you know from the text, which adjective best describes Danny?

    (a) lazy

    (b) clever

    (c) shy

    (d) sneaky

3 Using information from the text, explain why you chose the answer you did for #2.

_____

_____

_____

4 Explain the meaning of the title "A Little Ingenuity."

_____

_____

5 List in chronological order three events that happened in the text "The Lemonade Stand."

    a. _____

_____

    b. _____

_____

    c. _____

_____

6 What type of positive change or changes might Danny have made to his lemonade stand?

_____

_____

_____

7 What are two ways Danny's lemonade stand helped the yard-sale customers?

a. _____

b. _____

8 According to the text, which statement is something a young person needs to do when starting a business?

(a) Borrow money from the bank.

(b) Look for a need in the area where he or she lives.

(c) Take all the money you have saved and use it for your new business.

(d) Hire several employees and set yourself up as the boss.

9 Which phrase best defines the word *deterrents* as it is used in the following sentence?

Age and transportation to and from a place of employment can both be deterrents for young people hoping to find a way to make some money.

(a) something that prevents or inhibits

(b) something that adds growth

(c) something that embarrasses or humiliates

(d) something that takes time

10 Why might transportation be a problem for any young person trying to start a job or run a business?

_____

_____

_____

Time to Write!

Directions: Think about where you go to school. If you were allowed to start a business at your school, what is something you think the students or teachers there might need? Use the space below to write about your plan for a new business.

The idea I have for a new business at school is _____.

My school needs this because _____

_____

_____.

The people at school who would benefit most from this would be _____

_____.

They would benefit from this because _____

_____

_____.

These are the top three things I would need to get my new business started:

    a. _____

    b. _____

    c. _____

I would charge my customers the following prices:_____

_____.

I know these prices are fair and a good price to charge because _____

_____

_____.

The name of my new business would be _____.

Gross and Yuck

Melanie and her friends at camp were exhausted. They had spent the entire day doing a series of team events. Each cabin of girls competed against the other cabins to decide which one would win the camp trophy at the final ceremonies tonight. Melanie could not believe a week had already flown by at Camp Granger. It seemed as though she had only just arrived. She and the other girls had done all they could to secure a first-place victory for their group. She knew they would find out after supper if they were the winners or not. Last year, her cabin had lost by only five points. She hoped this year they had enough points to win.

All of the girls from Melanie's cabin wanted to take a short nap before the final ceremonies. They knew if they hurried, they had time to rest for about an hour before they would need to get ready. The competitions had been fun but also exhausting. Melanie and her best friend, Tina, had already had to come back to the cabin once today to get new socks and shoes. Their canoe had tipped over in the middle of the lake, and they had needed new outfits to be able to participate in the remaining events. Opening the door to the cabin, the six girls paraded through. Melanie was in the lead, but she came to an immediate stop as a horrible smell met the group of campers.

"What is that smell?" Tina yelled out before quickly covering her nose. "Gross! Yuck!" All of the other girls did the same. Only Melanie left hers uncovered as she tried to find the source of the offending smell.

"It's coming from under my bed," Melanie said as she leaned down to look. She pulled out the wet socks and shoes she and Tina had left in the cabin. "I think I've found the problem," Melanie said with a small grin. "Guess these should have gone outside with our wet clothes instead of inside." Melanie and Tina carried their wet things outside. One of the other girls sprayed the cabin with some of her perfume. The cabin didn't smell great, but it didn't smell as bad as it had when they'd first entered.

"Where are you two going?" one of the girls asked Melanie and Tina who were headed for the door. "To wash our feet," they both cried in unison.

We don't always smell good, but sometimes people smell the opposite of a rose. People use things like deodorant, perfumes, lotions, soaps, and shampoos to help them keep clean and smelling good. How often when you're getting nice and clean do you think about your feet or shoes? Have you taken a whiff of your shoes lately? If not, maybe you should. People do all sorts of things to be clean, but unfortunately, a lot of people don't do what they need to do to keep their little piggies smelling, well, not like barnyard animals.

So, why do people's feet and shoes smell bad sometimes? People are on their feet a lot. In fact, a lot of action happens to a person's feet each day. There's a lot of standing and sometimes running that happens. Most people spend a good portion of their day wearing socks and shoes. Have you ever taken off your socks or shoes after a long day at school or practice and wondered just for a minute what is making that horrible smell? Chances are it's all the bacteria working away on the bottom of your feet and inside your shoes.

Microscopic bacteria thrive in the environment created inside your socks and shoes. Most of the time you don't even realize these little creatures are there. When your feet get sweaty or wet and things start to heat up, these bacteria begin to really do their thing. They begin to multiply and eat the dead skin cells and oil found on your feet and inside your shoes. This process creates organic acids that release a smell. This natural process is what you know as the smell that comes from your stinky feet and shoes! Luckily for most people, the smell really isn't that bad. Only a small percent of the population ever gets the worst type of bacteria that causes the worst types of smells.

Everything may not smell like a rose, but with a bit of diligence at keeping your feet and shoes clean and dry, your feet can smell almost as good as a flower!

The following pages have questions based on the texts from Unit 21. You may look at the stories to help answer any questions. Use the back of the page if you need extra space for writing your answers.

1 Why are Melanie and her friends tired?

(a) They have been hiking.

(b) They have completed a list of chores.

(c) They have been competing in a series of games.

(d) They have stayed up too late each night at camp.

2 What problem do the girls face when they walk into their cabin?

(a) There is a horrible smell in the cabin.

(b) Other campers have been in their cabin.

(c) They left food sitting out in the cabin.

(d) Other campers put rotten eggs in their cabin.

3 What do the two texts have in common?

(a) bad smells

(b) nice people

(c) friendly teachers

(d) strange sights

4 List two items the text mentions that people may use to help them smell good.

a. _____

b. _____

5 Write two adjectives that could be used to describe something that has a bad odor or smell.

a. _____

b. _____

6 Which statement would be a correct inference about Melanie and her friends based on what you have learned from the story?

(a) They do not care if they win or lose in a competition.

(b) They do not get along well with the other campers.

(c) They are very competitive and like to win.

(d) They complain and often blame others for their problems.

7 Explain why Melanie and Tina are going to wash their feet.

_____

_____

8 Based on the text "Not Everything Smells Like a Rose," what is one cause of bad foot odor?

_____

9 List in chronological order three events that happened in the text "Gross and Yuck."

a. _____

_____

b. _____

_____

c. _____

_____

10 What does the word *microscopic* mean as it is used in the following sentence?

Microscopic bacteria thrive in the environment created inside your socks and shoes.

(a) miniscule

(b) colossal

(c) behemoth

(d) average

Time to Write!

Directions: Advertisers are masters at using words. They often use words to make you believe their product is the best. They use adjectives and clever phrases to make you believe you need what they are selling. Become a master at advertising, and use the space below to create a new cream that will fight foot odor. Be sure to include the following:

- Write the name of your new product on the tube.

- Add any designs or symbols you want to include on the product.

- Surround the picture with phrases and words that will convince people to buy your item.

- Include at least 5 fabulous phrases that will help sell your product.

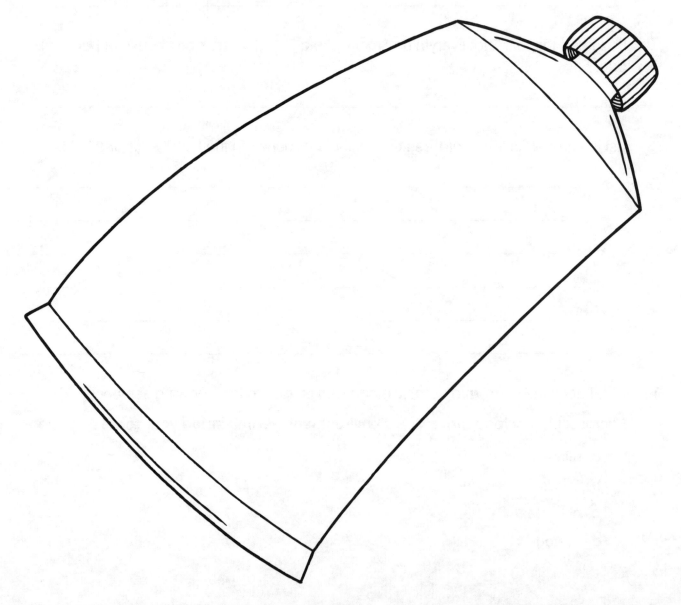

The Not So Itsy Bitsy Spider

Grant knew it was his job to go out and feed the family cat. His sister, Lynn, had fed her the night before. Grant had planned to go outside right after his own dinner and put Cooper's food in her dish, but after opening the back door and looking outside, he'd quickly returned back inside the house without leaving any food. He knew Cooper would be waiting for her meal. He knew she would be hungry. He needed to put the food in her dish, but he simply couldn't do it. There was no way he could feed the cat. Grant had arachnophobia. He was afraid of spiders, and hanging right over the cat's dish was an enormous spider's web. Grant stood in the kitchen, worrying about what to do next. He didn't want to ask his sister for help. He knew she would help him, but she had already taken her turn caring for their pet the night before. He didn't mind taking his turn. He loved their cat. Normally feeding her was not a problem.

After opening the door slowly, Grant looked outside again. The spider was still there, and Grant was certain the spider's web was getting larger. If he weren't so afraid of spiders, he knew he would marvel at the intricate design of the spider's web. He would be impressed by how quickly she worked and how adept the spider was at building her trap. He couldn't concentrate on any of these things, though, because he was afraid to take his eyes off the spider for fear he might not know where it went.

A loud meow came from the porch. Cooper sat there, staring at Grant. He knew she was waiting for him to pour her food into the bowl. He thought about getting a new bowl and trying to convince Cooper to eat from it, but he knew the cat was too picky to change her routine. She would refuse to eat it, and he would feel even guiltier about her not getting her evening meal. Grant was about to go inside and ask his sister for help, when Cooper made a surprising move. She pushed her dish with her paw and continued to bat at it until she had moved it closer to Grant and further away from the spider. Grant could not believe his eyes! It was almost like Cooper knew he was afraid and had done what she could to help him. Grant poured Cooper's food into the bowl, and her answering purr was all he needed to hear.

Everyone is afraid sometimes. Some people do not like the dark. Others are afraid of snakes or spiders. Still other people have a fear of clowns. It is okay to be afraid, but some fears are so extreme that people who have them have a hard time dealing with their fears. These extreme fears are known as phobias. Imagine, for example, that you have such an extreme fear of clowns that you cannot go into a store because there is a doll that looks like a clown. When a fear stops someone from doing something that he or she might otherwise want to do, the fear becomes a phobia.

There are many different types of phobias. One type is agoraphobia. People who have agoraphobia worry about having panic attacks in public places. A panic attack can cause people to have very real physical symptoms. These symptoms can include difficulty breathing, feelings of dizziness, and uncontrollable shaking. Panic attacks rarely last for very long, but this is not always a comfort to the person experiencing these feelings.

Another type of phobia is the fear of being in tight or enclosed spaces. This phobia is known as claustrophobia. Many people who have claustrophobia have a hard time doing things like riding in an elevator or being in a small room with a crowd of people. Like other phobias, claustrophobia can often limit the things people can do because they will avoid any situation where they might feel the space is too small.

No one knows exactly why some people have phobias while others do not. People with phobias can get help. There are many different treatments available to help people work through their fears. Maybe someday people will be able to overcome all different types of phobias and live in a world with little to fear.

UNIT 22 QUESTIONS

Name

Date

The following pages have questions based on the texts from Unit 22. You may look at the stories to help answer any questions. Use the back of the page if you need extra space for writing your answers.

1 What type of phobia does Grant have?

(a) claustrophobia

(b) social phobia

(c) agoraphobia

(d) arachnophobia

2 What do the two texts have in common?

_____

_____

_____

_____

3 How is Cooper able to help Grant?

(a) The cat kills the spider.

(b) The cat runs in the house and gets Grant's sister.

(c) The cat knocks down the spider's web.

(d) The cat moves the dish away from the spider's web.

4 Using evidence from the text, explain how phobias are different than fears.

_____

_____

_____

5 Which statement is true?

(a) There is only one type of phobia.

(b) People cannot be cured from their phobias.

(c) Someone with claustrophobia feels safe in small, crowded places.

(d) A phobia is an extreme type of fear.

6   What led to Grant being unable to feed the cat when he first tried to feed her?

_____

_____

7   Which statement is false about panic attacks?

(a) Panic attacks happen only to people after they reach the age of fifty.

(b) Panic attacks can cause real physical symptoms.

(c) Panic attacks can be triggered by phobias.

(d) Panic attacks can cause a person to have difficulty breathing.

8   List in chronological order three things that happened in the text "The Not So Itsy Bitsy Spider."

a. _____

b. _____

c. _____

9   Write two questions you would like to have answered about phobias.

a. _____

_____

b. _____

_____

10 With your teacher's permission, use the Internet or other sources to find the answers to the questions you wrote for #9. Write the answers to each question on the lines below. If you are unable to do research, write what you think the answers are.

a. _____

_____

b. _____

_____

Time to Write!

Directions: Imagine you have a friend who suffers from acrophobia, which is a fear of heights. Write a letter to your friend explaining why he or she should not be afraid. Do not say anything mean or put down your friend for having this fear. Be supportive and caring in your letter. You might even want to do some research about acrophobia before beginning your letter.

Dear Friend,

_____

_____

_____

_____

_____

_____

_____

_____

_____

_____

_____

_____

Sincerely,

_____

Something Extra: Think about a time you were afraid. Write about the experience on the back of the page. Be sure to explain what you were afraid of and why you felt afraid.

Brace Yourself

"What do you need to tell me, Mom?" Lacey asked her mother.

Lacey's mom motioned for her to sit down on the couch beside her. She turned to Lacey and said, "You might want to brace yourself for this. Oh, wait. That's probably a bad choice of words."

"Just tell me whatever you need to tell me, Mom. I can handle it." Lacey knew she was only in the fifth grade, but people were always telling her how mature she was for her age.

"The orthodontist said it's certain that your sister doesn't need braces, but you are going to have to get them."

"What!" Lacey couldn't believe it. Twins were supposed to share everything. How could she need them, but Tracey didn't?

"I know this is probably a little hard to swallow," her mother began. "Oh my, I keep saying all the wrong things, don't I? Anyway, honey, it will only be for a couple of years, and then your teeth will be perfectly straight. Isn't that good news?"

Lacey tried to think. She guessed braces wouldn't be horrible. After all, half the other students in her class already had them. Most of them liked going to the orthodontist. At least now she could join in on all the conversations they had at lunch about their braces.

"Okay, Mom. You don't have to worry. I'll em*brace* this change like I know you want me to do."

Lacey's mother grinned at her daughter's obvious pun before wrapping her in a giant hug.

Perfect Smiles

As people grow up, they lose their first set of teeth. These first teeth are usually known as baby teeth. These baby teeth are eventually all replaced by a permanent set of teeth that most people will keep for the rest of their lives. For some people, these teeth will come in perfectly straight, and there will be no problems. Other people will find that their new teeth do not seem to fit as well in their mouths as their baby teeth did. When this happens, many people seek help from an orthodontist.

Orthodontists are trained to deal with many different problems involving the alignment of a person's teeth. Some people have crooked teeth that need to be straightened. These crooked teeth are generally corrected when a person wears braces for a continuous length of time. For some people, the time can be as short as six months. For others, the braces may need to remain for several years. Once a person has removed the braces, a retainer is usually worn to keep the teeth from shifting once again.

Orthodontists also work with patients to correct problems with their bite. If a person's jaw does not line up correctly, this can cause a person to also have issues with his or her teeth. Teeth that are straight are easier for a person to clean. This also helps prevent problems such as gum disease and cavities.

There are some people who do not like going to the dentist, but the dentist is the first person to look at a person's teeth. The dentist will take X-rays and watch how a person's teeth are lining up in his or her mouth once all of the baby teeth have been lost. It is the dentist who generally makes the first recommendation that someone seek the help of an orthodontist. Regardless of which one you see first, both the dentist and the orthodontist work hard to make sure everyone has a perfect smile.

UNIT 23 QUESTIONS

Name

Date

The following pages have questions based on the texts from Unit 23. You may look at the stories to help answer any questions. Use the back of the page if you need extra space for writing your answers.

1 What news does Lacey's mother have to tell Lacey?

(a) She needs to get glasses.

(b) The family is moving to another state.

(c) Lacey's twin sister has made the volleyball team.

(d) Lacey needs to get braces, but her twin sister does not.

2 Why does Lacey decide braces won't be that bad to have?

_____

_____

_____

3 What is one reason someone might need to see an orthodontist?

(a) to get braces

(b) to get an eye exam

(c) to have a cavity filled

(d) to get a dental checkup

4 How long will a person have to wear braces?

(a) six months

(b) two to three years

(c) every night

(d) Length of time varies.

5 Explain why the text was titled "Brace Yourself."

_____

_____

_____

_____

UNIT 23 QUESTIONS | **Name** | **Date**

6 Write a sentence from the text that best explains how Lacey feels about getting braces at the beginning of the story.

_____

_____

_____

7 How do you know Lacey's feelings have changed by the end of the story?

_____

_____

_____

8 What do the two texts have in common?

(a) orthodontics

(b) exercise

(c) school

(d) entertainment

9 Give one reason from the text why it is beneficial or good for people to have straight teeth.

_____

_____

_____

10 Which statement is not a fact?

(a) As people grow up, they lose their first set of teeth.

(b) Orthodontists also work with patients to correct problems with their bite.

(c) It is the dentist who generally makes the first recommendation that someone seek the help of an orthodontist.

(d) Everyone wants a perfect smile.

©*Teacher Created Resources*   123   *#3895 Nonfiction & Fiction Paired Texts*

Time to Write!

Directions: Most people want a perfect smile, and most people like having something to smile about each day. Think about what makes you smile. Write a list of five things that make you smile. Then explain why each thing makes you happy.

Things That Make Me Smile

1. _____ makes me smile. This makes me smile because

_____

_____.

2. _____ makes me smile. This makes me smile because

_____

_____.

3. _____ makes me smile. This makes me smile because

_____

_____.

4. _____ makes me smile. This makes me smile because

_____

_____.

5. _____ makes me smile. This makes me smile because

_____

_____.

Laura was sick. Her runny nose and cough were bad, but they were not the symptoms that had kept her home from school. When her mother had come into her room to wake her up for school, she'd said Laura felt hot. She took her temperature and found out that Laura had a fever. Her mother had tucked her back into her bed and told her a fever meant she could not go to school. This was not good news to her. Today, her class was having a party, and she was going to miss it.

For weeks, Laura's class had been in competition with the other fifth-grade classes at her school. They were trying to see who could bring in the most plastic bottles to donate to the recycling center. Their teacher had been doing a unit on recycling. They'd learned how important it was to not throw things like aluminum cans and plastic water bottles in the trash. These items could be easily recycled, and if everyone would learn to do this, it would help save the planet from so much trash.

Laura had taken the challenge seriously. She wanted to learn to recycle and, of course, she wanted her class to win the challenge. On Friday, the entire class had listened attentively as the principal's voice came over the speaker and announced to the school that their class had won! Everyone had cheered, and Mr. Morgan had announced the celebration party would be on Monday. Laura had cheered along with the rest of the class. She hadn't known then that she wouldn't be able to attend.

After three days of being sick, Laura was finally able to go back to school. The doctor had explained to her that she had gotten a virus but that she was fine to go back to school once she was feeling better. Laura's mother had called ahead to the school to let them know when she would return. As Laura walked into her room, she thought it was strange because all of the lights were out. Then she heard everyone shout the word *surprise*, and the lights were switched on. A big banner hung across the back wall of the classroom that read, "Welcome Back, Laura. We Didn't Want to Celebrate Without You!"

The Invaders

No one likes being sick. It feels terrible to have a runny nose, a horrible cough, or a high fever. When people are sick, they usually do not feel like doing any of the things they might normally do. Sometimes, being sick even keeps people from being able to participate in special celebrations or activities. So, if being sick is such a bad thing, why do people get sick?

People don't choose to get sick. Try to imagine that your body is constantly having to fight off invaders. These microscopic invaders are called germs. You can't see them by looking with your regular eye. You would need a microscope to get a good look at the little beasties that try to make you sick. Your body, however, is an amazing machine, and each day, it fights off different germs that try to make you sick. Most people know how to help fight germs by doing simple, everyday things like washing their hands with warm water and plenty of soap or covering their mouths when they cough or sneeze. All of these actions will help people stay healthy. Sometimes germs still manage to be successful in their efforts, and they manage to invade and make someone sick.

There are four major types of germs that often affect people in a negative way. Bacteria, fungi, viruses, and protozoa are all invaders that can cause problems in the human body. Bacteria can cause infections inside the body. However, the human body also needs some types of bacteria to do its job effectively. Bacteria are needed to help break down waste products in the human body. The other types of germs also cause their share of problems. A fungus loves to live in damp, wet places. This is why many athletes get a fungus between their toes known as athlete's foot. Viruses also cause their share of problems, spreading things like the flu and chicken pox. Finally, protozoa usually hide out in water. They can cause severe stomach pains.

So, what can a person do to be protected against such aggressive invaders? Practice those simple rules of washing your hands, keeping things clean, and keeping your germs to yourself when you cough or sneeze. Maybe with a little effort, we can all win against these tiny invaders.

The following pages have questions based on the texts from Unit 24. You may look at the stories to help answer any questions. Use the back of the page if you need extra space for writing your answers.

1 Why did Laura's mother tell her she could not go to school?

    ⓐ It was Saturday.

    ⓑ She was sick with a fever.

    ⓒ Her teacher was going to be absent.

    ⓓ She had missed the bus.

2 What type of contest did Laura's class win?

    ⓐ a school-spirit contest

    ⓑ a math contest

    ⓒ a science contest

    ⓓ a recycling contest

3 Which statement is true according to the text?

    ⓐ People can choose whether they get sick.

    ⓑ Washing your hands in cold water is as good as washing your hands in warm water.

    ⓒ Some types of bacteria are actually good for your body.

    ⓓ People can't win in the fight against germs.

4 Explain why Laura's class did not have the party until she returned to school.

_____

_____

_____

5 List the four major types of germs.

    a. _____

    b. _____

    c. _____

    d. _____

6 If Laura's class were involved in another contest, what would Laura most likely do?

    (a) refuse to participate

    (b) work hard to help her class win

    (c) skip school so she would not have to help

    (d) tell everyone she was the only person who could participate

7 What do the two texts have in common?

    (a) celebrations

    (b) germs

    (c) school

    (d) recycling

8 List in chronological order three events that happened in the text "Sick Day."

    a. _____

    _____

    b. _____

    _____

    c. _____

    _____

9 Which statement is an opinion?

    (a) No one likes being sick.

    (b) You need a microscope to be able to see any germs.

    (c) Some germs cause people to get high fevers.

    (d) There are four major types of germs.

10 List some things you can do at home or school to help stop the spread of germs.

_____

_____

_____

 **Name** **Date**

Time to Write!

Directions: Chicken pox is a disease that once affected many children. Luckily, a vaccine was discovered for this disease. Most young children receive vaccines to protect them from many different illnesses. With help from your teacher, research chicken pox. Use book sources or the Internet to find out more about this disease. Once you've done your research, list six things you learned about chicken pox.

Chicken Pox

1. _____

   _____

2. _____

   _____

3. _____

   _____

4. _____

   _____

5. _____

   _____

6. _____

   _____

Something Extra: Look up the definition for the word *vaccine*. Read over the definition and then rewrite it using your own words.

A vaccine is _____

_____.

The Talk

Justin wanted to talk to his grandfather. He had something on his mind, but he didn't quite know what he should say to him. He had been thinking a lot about his grandfather's health. It had really been bothering him ever since his class at school had started a unit on living healthier lives. His fifth-grade teacher had gone over things like the importance of exercise and making good food choices. They'd studied the food pyramid, too. But there was also one more thing she had talked about that was important for people to do to lead healthier lives. She taught the class that part of living a healthy life was doing so without any tobacco products. Justin knew his grandfather smoked cigarettes, even though he didn't smoke around any of the grandchildren. He wanted to talk to him about what he had learned, but he did not want to seem disrespectful. He didn't know what to do. He loved his grandfather very much, but he also knew it was hard for people to get rid of bad habits, even if they loved the person who asked them to stop.

Taking a deep breath, Justin knocked on the door of his grandfather's shop. He heard the familiar voice holler for him to come in. "Justin," his grandfather said when he saw who his visitor was, "I was just thinking about you. I was wondering when you were going to show up so we could start working on that wooden racecar of yours. When I was a little boy, I worked on my car in this same shop with my father. I can't even remember if we won a ribbon once we raced it, but I remember how much fun it was working with my dad. I wish your dad could be here, Justin. I know it's hard for you that he is deployed right now, but you know I'm here whenever you need me."

"Grandpa, I need to ask you something," Justin began, the words rushing from him. "We've been studying the bad effects of using tobacco. I know you smoke, but I don't want anything bad to ever happen to you." Justin watched as the corners of his grandfather's mouth turned up in a smile.

"I've got something to show you, Justin," he said. Then he rolled up one sleeve on his shirt. On his arm was a square patch that looked like a bandage. "It's a special patch from the doctor to help me quit smoking. I'm going to try my hardest, Justin, for you and for me."

Tobacco use is an addiction that is hard for people to stop. What is an addiction? An addiction is something you crave or want to do even when you know it may not be good for you. Smoking cigarettes is one addiction that cannot only hurt you, but it can also harm those around you. The smoke from cigarettes can cause problems for those who live with or spend time near people who smoke.

Sadly, every single day, over 3,000 children between the ages of twelve and seventeen will begin to smoke. Despite this alarming statistic, the news that smoking is bad for a person seems to be reaching the ears of those listening. There are fewer people smoking today than in the past. Yet, with all the information about how smoking can hurt a person or even others near the smoker, why would someone ever start smoking?

There are many different reasons why someone might start smoking. For some children, doing the opposite of what they are told is appealing. Others may start because someone they already know smokes. This person may even be someone they admire, and so they are emulating what the other person is doing. There are even a few younger people who mistakenly believe smoking makes them look grown up, so that is why they try that first cigarette. Many still don't realize how difficult it will be to stop using tobacco once they start.

So why should people refrain from using tobacco products? There are many reasons, but most of these involve a person's health. Smoking can cause bad breath. A person who smokes will also begin to have discolored teeth. There is an odor that often clings to the clothes of the smoker or those who live with someone who smokes. Smokers tend to have more colds and coughs than those who don't use tobacco. Since smoking can affect a person's ability to breathe, it's often difficult for someone who smokes to keep up with those who don't smoke when participating in different activities. Finally, smoking can lead to other serious, life-threatening illnesses. Obviously, smoking can be a hard addiction to quit, but it can be done; however, the easiest way to stop is simply to never start.

The following pages have questions based on the texts from Unit 25. You may look at the stories to help answer any questions. Use the back of the page if you need extra space for writing your answers.

1 What event caused Justin to want to speak to his grandfather?

    (a) A friend of his was hurt in a car accident.

    (b) He had learned at school how harmful using tobacco is.

    (c) His mother asked him to talk to his grandfather.

    (d) He had to interview his grandfather for an assignment at school.

2 Write the sentence from the text that explains why Justin is hesitant to speak to his grandfather.

_____

_____

_____

_____

3 What do the two texts have in common?

    (a) following the food pyramid

    (b) stopping the use of tobacco

    (c) following the rules of the classroom

    (d) communicating with family members

4 Using information from the text "Addiction," explain what the word *addiction* means.

_____

_____

_____

5 Which word is a characteristic that could be used to describe Justin?

    (a) secretive

    (b) sly

    (c) caring

    (d) sneaky

6 List two reasons why someone might start smoking.

a. _____

b. _____

7 Based on information from the text, which statement is true?

a There are more people smoking today than ever.

b Fewer people smoke today than they did in the past.

c The number of people smoking has not changed very much in the past few decades.

d There are more teenage smokers than there are adult smokers.

8 Using information from the text, list two effects of smoking.

a. _____

b. _____

9 Based on what you know about Justin's character, if one of his friends wanted to start smoking, what would Justin most likely do? Explain why you believe he would react this way.

_____

_____

_____

_____

_____

_____

10 According to the texts, what is the easiest way to stop smoking?

_____

_____

_____

Time to Write!

Part 1

Directions: Brainstorm some ideas that you believe are part of an unhealthy lifestyle. Write your ideas in the space below.

Part 2

Directions: Circle one of your ideas in Part 1. Use this idea to write a short speech to convince people to no longer engage or participate in this unhealthy behavior. Use persuasive words and phrases to get others to agree with you. Be sure to give suggestions that will help people know what they need to do to stop the unhealthy behavior and start some healthy habits instead.

Ideas for Leading a Healthy Lifestyle

_____

_____

_____

_____

_____

_____

_____

The Artist

"What is that?" Steven leaned over his brother's shoulder and peered at the picture he was drawing.

Drake sighed. "I am terrible at this; I can't draw. My assignment for art class tomorrow is to try replicating a famous painting. I don't think I'll ever get it right."

"It's not that bad," Steven said. "I can tell now that you're trying to draw the *Mona Lisa*. That's a famous portrait you're trying to copy, you know. Everyone talks about her smile. You've drawn the long hair around her face, and her eyes look good, but there's something not quite right about her mouth."

"What do you think I should do?" Drake asked his brother.

"Well, for one thing, I don't think you should try to draw it from your memory. You should be looking at a copy of the painting. Let me help you pull up a copy on the Internet." Steven pulled out his phone and started searching for a copy. He typed in the artist's name, Leonardo da Vinci. Then he searched for the famous painting. Within seconds, he had an image for Drake to look at while he tried to draw the painting.

"Thanks, Steven," Drake said. "I don't know why I didn't think of that." Drake began drawing again. "Tomorrow, we are going to work on a report about Leonardo's life. My teacher wants us to study five different artists and know what their most famous works are. She told us Leonardo da Vinci did other things besides painting. Apparently, he was good at doing a lot of different things." Drake looked at his picture and sighed again. "Drawing is definitely something I am not good at. It's a good thing there are other things I can do well."

"I think you're doing much better now," Stephen said, "but you do see what you were doing wrong now, don't you?" Drake's cheeks turned a slight shade of pink at his brother's teasing.

"Yes, I see. In the original painting, she is smiling with her mouth closed."

"And?" Stephen prompted Drake.

"And she doesn't have braces!"

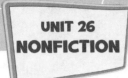
Leonardo da Vinci

Leonardo da Vinci was born in 1452. This period of time became known as the Italian Renaissance. The word *renaissance* means rebirth. There were so many changes happening in Europe during this time that it was like a new beginning as people began to show a great interest in science and the arts. Leonardo da Vinci was a man who was interested in both of these subjects. He was truly a Renaissance man.

Many people know Leonardo da Vinci as a painter. His most famous painting is the *Mona Lisa*. Leonardo was good at many other things besides painting. He had a true interest in how things worked. He was especially fascinated by how things worked in nature. He would conduct experiments to try to understand the world around him. Leonardo was especially interested in studying anatomy, or how the body is made. He drew detailed pictures of the human body and was accurate with his sketches. His talent as an artist helped him as a scientist because he was able to make detailed sketches along with the notes he wrote whenever he studied something new. Anyone who looked at Leonardo's notes might have had a hard time reading his words. He wrote backwards, or from right to left. As someone who wrote left-handed, he said he found it easier to write in this direction.

Another talent Leonardo was famous for was his skill in designing. He was so good at designing things that the Italian government asked him to help design new weapons for the country. He made many improvements to some weapons that already existed. One interesting design he worked on was the idea for creating a tank. The idea for this weapon was so ahead of his time that no one living in his century knew how to build the advanced weapon.

Leonardo da Vinci died in 1519. He was recognized as a man of great talents during his lifetime. He will always be remembered as a true Renaissance man.

The following pages have questions based on the texts from Unit 26. You may look at the stories to help answer any questions. Use the back of the page if you need extra space for writing your answers.

1 Why is Drake upset about his homework assignment?

(a) He does not want to do a report on an artist.

(b) He cannot draw as well as his brother.

(c) He does not want to do any homework.

(d) He does not think he can draw well.

2 What do the two texts have in common?

(a) Both are about doing well in school.

(b) Both are about a famous artist.

(c) Both are about a well-known author.

(d) Both are about helping other people.

3 Which paragraph of the text "Leonardo da Vinci" best explains the meaning of the word *renaissance*?

(a) paragraph 1

(b) paragraph 2

(c) paragraph 3

(d) paragraph 4

4 According to the text, what does the word *renaissance* mean?

_____

_____

5 List in chronological order three events that happened in the text "The Artist."

a. _____

_____

b. _____

_____

c. _____

_____

6 Based on information from the text, write two facts about Leonardo da Vinci.

a. _____

_____

b. _____

_____

7 At the end of the story, why is Drake embarrassed?

(a) He knew he couldn't draw as well as his brother, Steven.

(b) He found out the woman in the original picture did not have braces.

(c) He had forgotten to do all of his homework.

(d) He did not have the supplies he needed to finish his work.

8 According to the text, why might someone have trouble reading notes written by Leonardo da Vinci?

_____

_____

_____

9 Which future weapon did Leonardo da Vinci envision?

(a) a machine gun

(b) a stick of dynamite

(c) a tank

(d) a submarine

10 Use evidence from the text and explain how you know Drake and Steven are brothers who care about each other.

_____

_____

_____

Time to Write!

Directions: Leonardo da Vinci lived from 1452–1519. He lived near or during the same time as many other well-known people in history. Choose a name from the list in the box. Research the person using the Internet or other sources. Then complete the section below.

Michelangelo	**William Shakespeare**
Galileo Galilei	**Ferdinand Magellan**
Johannes Gutenberg	**Christopher Columbus**

I chose this person: _____

He was born in this year: _____

He is famous because _____

_____.

Four facts I learned are as follows:

Fact 1: _____

_____

Fact 2: _____

_____

Fact 3: _____

_____

Fact 4: _____

_____

Something I didn't find out that I wish I knew about this person is _____

_____

_____.

Answer Key

Unit 1
1. b
2. c
3. He is afraid he will catch the disease.
4. Answers may include the following: He was scared. He obviously had not been given the vaccination. Would he catch the disease?
5. a
6. The scar was caused from a scab that formed after getting the vaccination.
7. the ability to fight a disease
8. c
9. Answers may include the following: sores or pox on a person's body, horrible scarring, and blindness.
10. a

Unit 2
1. a
2. The scheduled after-school jazz band practice had been over for nearly thirty minutes, but Margaret and four of her friends had begged Mr. Potts to stay for a little longer.
3. c
4. b
5. b
6. Answers will vary.
7. d
8. someone who uses their money to help others
9. a
10. Both are about women named Margaret who act as heroes and show courage in the face of danger.

Unit 3
1. c
2. d
3. Answers will vary.
4. a
5. b
6. She understands that the "arms race" is about weapons and not human arms.
7. Each wanted to have bigger and better super bombs. They also wanted to be able to defend themselves against each other.
8. c
9. a
10. Answers will vary.

Unit 4
1. d
2. a
3. b
4.–6. Answers will vary.
7. d
8. Answers may include the following: Everyone had agreed it was a great idea. The thought of making the scrapbook made cleaning out the basement more like a craft project and kept Corinne from being sad.
9. a
10. Answers will vary.

Unit 5
1. a
2. Answers may include the following: She was the only one who was passionate about tennis. She couldn't imagine her life without playing the game.
3. a

4. d
5. Answers will vary.
6. c
7. Both are about women playing tennis. Both are about females being able to play as well as or better than males.
8.–10. Answers will vary.

Unit 6
1. d
2. Answers will vary.
3. c
4. They missed the beginning of the program that explained it was fiction.
5. c
6. Answers will vary.
7. c
8. Answers will vary.
9. b
10. Answers will vary.

Unit 7
1. b
2. a
3. b
4.–7. Answers will vary.
8. c
9.–10. Answers will vary.

Unit 8
1. b
2. Answers will vary.
3. d
4. Answers may include the following: Children long ago were not required to go to school and usually had to work outside the home.
5. Answers will vary.
6. c
7. c
8. a
9.–10. Answers will vary.

Unit 9
1. a
2. a
3. President Theodore "Teddy" Roosevelt
4. b
5. Answers will vary.
6. d
7. d
8. Answers may include the following: Political cartoonists heard the story and drew pictures of Roosevelt refusing to shoot the bear. Eventually, the bear in the cartoons became smaller as new ones were drawn, and the bear in the picture became the size of a cub.
9. Answers will vary but could include that people might feel more compassion for a young cub.
10. Answers will vary.

Unit 10
1. d
2. He smells smoke.
3. Answers will vary but could include the sense of sight. He sees the fire at his next-door neighbor's house or the sense of hearing when his father tells him what he sees out the window.

4. c

5. He could smell smoke.

6. a

7. b

8. a

9.–10. Answers will vary.

Unit 11

1. b

2. c

3. Animals that are nocturnal are active during the night hours rather than during the day.

4. b

5. b

6. b

7. a

8. They attract the nighttime creatures at night by reflecting the light of the moon better.

9. bats and moths

10. c

Unit 12

1. b

2. Answers will vary.

3. Both are about eagles.

4. c

5. Answers will vary.

6. "Live in harmony" means to get along peacefully.

7. money and the Great Seal

8. Answers will vary.

9. Sentence choices will vary depending on answer for #8.

10. a

Unit 13

1. b

2. b

3. b

4. moved faster

5. a

6. a

7. a

8. c

9. He was amazed at what his mother could do with a needle and thread.

10. c

Unit 14

1. c

2. Answers will vary but could include the following: There is a continuous source of water. The water helps crops to grow. There is a continuous source of food.

3. a

4. People can get water and food from other sources. People have better transportation than in the past and other methods besides using rivers.

5. d

6. Answers may include the following: He overslept and missed breakfast, so his stomach is growling. He cannot concentrate in class.

7. a

8. b

9. the importance of having a food source easily available

10. Answers will vary.

Unit 15

1. a

2. b

3. Answers may include the following: Both are about not having enough money for things and thinking about the differences between what a person needs for survival rather than things they simply want.

4. This means they would pay for an item over several payments rather than paying all at once for a purchase.

5. d

6. Answers may include the following: He cares about his brother and wants to help him, he wants to play the game, too.

7. d

8. Answers may include the following: The period in history has become known as the Great Depression. This period lasted throughout the decade of the 1930s.

9. Answers will vary.

10. b

Unit 16

1. c

2. Heather wants others to find happiness from the shells, so she leaves them. Also, she is determined to find the owner of the ring.

3. b

4. c

5. Answers will vary but could include that there is sentimental worth attached to the ring.

6. b

7. b

8.–9. Answers will vary.

10. b

Unit 17

1. a

2. c

3. a

4. the ones she keeps in her mind

5. No matter where she is or what she is doing, she can look at them.

6. Answers may include the following: They are both photographers, or they both take pictures that document or show what is going on around them.

7. Answers will vary.

8. c

9.–10. Answers will vary.

Unit 18

1. b

2. d

3. They were excited about seeing the whales and enjoyed their mother's surprise.

4. c

5. no longer exist

6. a

7. Some people may not agree with the statement. It cannot be proven true.

8. c

9. The smaller size helps them to move quickly.

10. She has a secretive smile on her face as she looks at the children. She is not saying a lot about the trip they are taking.

Answer Key (cont.)

Unit 19
1. d
2. She is trying to take care of her mother.
3. b
4. She uses the light from the refrigerator so she can see.
5. b
6. a
7. b
8. Answers will vary.
9. People do not stop working; they do not get enough sleep.
10. b

Unit 20
1. Both are about younger people finding ways to make money.
2. b
3. He pays attention to the people talking and watches how they are behaving, and he realizes there is a need for a place for people to get something to drink and find some shade. He uses this to make money at the sale.
4. By being clever, a young person can make money.
5.–6. Answers will vary.
7. Answers may include the following: The customers had shade, a place to get something to drink, and a place to rest.
8. b
9. a
10. Many young people can't go somewhere to work because they do not have a way or transportation to get to a job.

Unit 21
1. c
2. a
3. a
4. Answers may include the following: lotion, perfume, soap, deodorant, and shampoo.
5. Answers will vary.
6. c
7. They realize if their socks and shoes smell that bad, then their feet probably smell the same.
8.–9. Answers will vary.
10. a

Unit 22
1. d
2. They are both about extreme fears or phobias.
3. d
4. The text states that when a fear stops someone from doing something that he or she might otherwise want to do, the fear becomes a phobia.
5. d
6. There was a spider near the cat's food dish.
7. a
8.–10. Answers will vary.

Unit 23
1. d
2. Many of her classmates already have them. She will be able to join in on their conversations about braces.
3. a
4. d

5. The title is a pun with the word *brace* because the main character is getting braces, and her mother knew she would need to "brace" herself for the news that she had to get them.
6.–7. Answers will vary.
8. a
9. Answers may include the following: Straight teeth are easier to clean and do not get cavities as easily. Having straight teeth helps prevent gum disease.
10. d

Unit 24
1. b
2. d
3. c
4. They knew she was a big part of why they won the contest, so they wanted to wait for her to return to school.
5. (Answers can be in any order.) bacteria, fungi, viruses, protozoa
6. b
7. b
8. Answers will vary.
9. a
10. Answers may include the following: washing your hands with warm water, covering your mouth when you cough or sneeze, and keeping both you and your home clean.

Unit 25
1. b
2. He wanted to talk to him about what he had learned, but he did not want to seem disrespectful.
3. b
4. An addiction is something you crave or want to do even when you know it may not be good for you.
5. c
6. Answers may include the following: to do something that is different than what they are supposed to do, because they think it makes them appear older, and because someone they know or admire uses tobacco.
7. b
8. Answers may include the following: bad breath, discolored teeth, bad odor, more colds and coughs, serious illness, problems breathing, and life-long addiction.
9. He would try and talk them out of smoking because he was willing to talk to his grandfather about quitting and leading a healthier lifestyle, so he would do the same for a friend.
10. never start

Unit 26
1. d
2. b
3. a
4. rebirth
5.–6. Answers will vary.
7. b
8. He wrote backwards because he was left-handed and felt it was easier to write that way.
9. c
10. Answers will vary.

Meeting Standards

Each passage and activity meets one or more of the following Common Core State Standards ©
Copyright 2010. National Governors Association Center for Best Practices and Council of Chief State
School Officers. All rights reserved. For more information about the Common Core State Standards, go
to *http://www.corestandards.org/* or *http://www.teachercreated.com/standards/*.

Reading: Literature	Passages and Activities
Key Ideas and Details	
ELA.RL.5.1: Quote accurately from a text when explaining what the text says explicity and when drawing inferences from the text.	All fiction
Craft and Structure	
ELA.RL.5.4: Determine the meaning of words and phrases as they are used in a text, including figurative language such as metaphors and similies.	All fiction
Range of Reading and Level of Text Complexity	
ELA.RL.5.10: By the end of the year, read and comprehend literature, including stories, dramas, and poetry, at the high end of the grades 4–5 text complexity band independently and proficiently.	All fiction
Reading: Informational Text	**Passages and Activities**
Key Ideas and Details	
ELA.RI.5.1: Quote accurately from a text when explaining what the text says explicitly and when drawing inferences from the text.	All nonfiction
Craft and Structure	
ELA.RI.5.4: Determine the meaning of general academic and domain-specific words and phrases in a text relevant to a *grade 5 topic or subject area.*	All nonfiction

Meeting Standards *(cont.)*

Integration of Knowledge and Ideas	
ELA.RI.5.8: Explain how an author uses reasons and evidence to support particular points in a text, identifying which reasons and evidence support which point(s).	All nonfiction

Range of Reading and Level of Text Complexity	
ELA.RI.5.10: By the end of the year, read and comprehend informational texts, including history/social studies, science, and technical texts, at the high end of the grades 4–5 text complexity band independently and proficiently.	All nonfiction

Writing	**Passages and Activities**
Text Types and Purposes	
ELA.W.5.1: Write opinion pieces on topics or texts, supporting a point of view with reasons and information.	**Unit** 5, Unit 8, Unit 23, Unit 25
ELA.W.5.2: Write informative/explanatory texts to examine a topic and convey ideas and information clearly.	**Unit** 2, Unit 6, Unit 9, Unit 12, Unit 15, Unit 16, Unit 20, Unit 21, Unit 22
ELA.W.5.3: Write narratives to develop real or imagined experiences or events using effective technique, descriptive details, and clear event sequences.	**Unit** 3, Unit 4, Unit 11, Unit 18, Unit 19
Production and Distribution of Writing	
ELA.W.5.4: Produce clear and coherent writing in which the development and organization are appropriate to task, purpose, and audience.	All units
Research to Build and Present Knowledge	
ELA.W.5.7: Conduct short research projects that use several sources to build knowledge through investigation of different aspects of a topic.	Unit 1, Unit 4, Unit 10, Unit 13, Unit 14, Unit 17, Unit 24, Unit 26